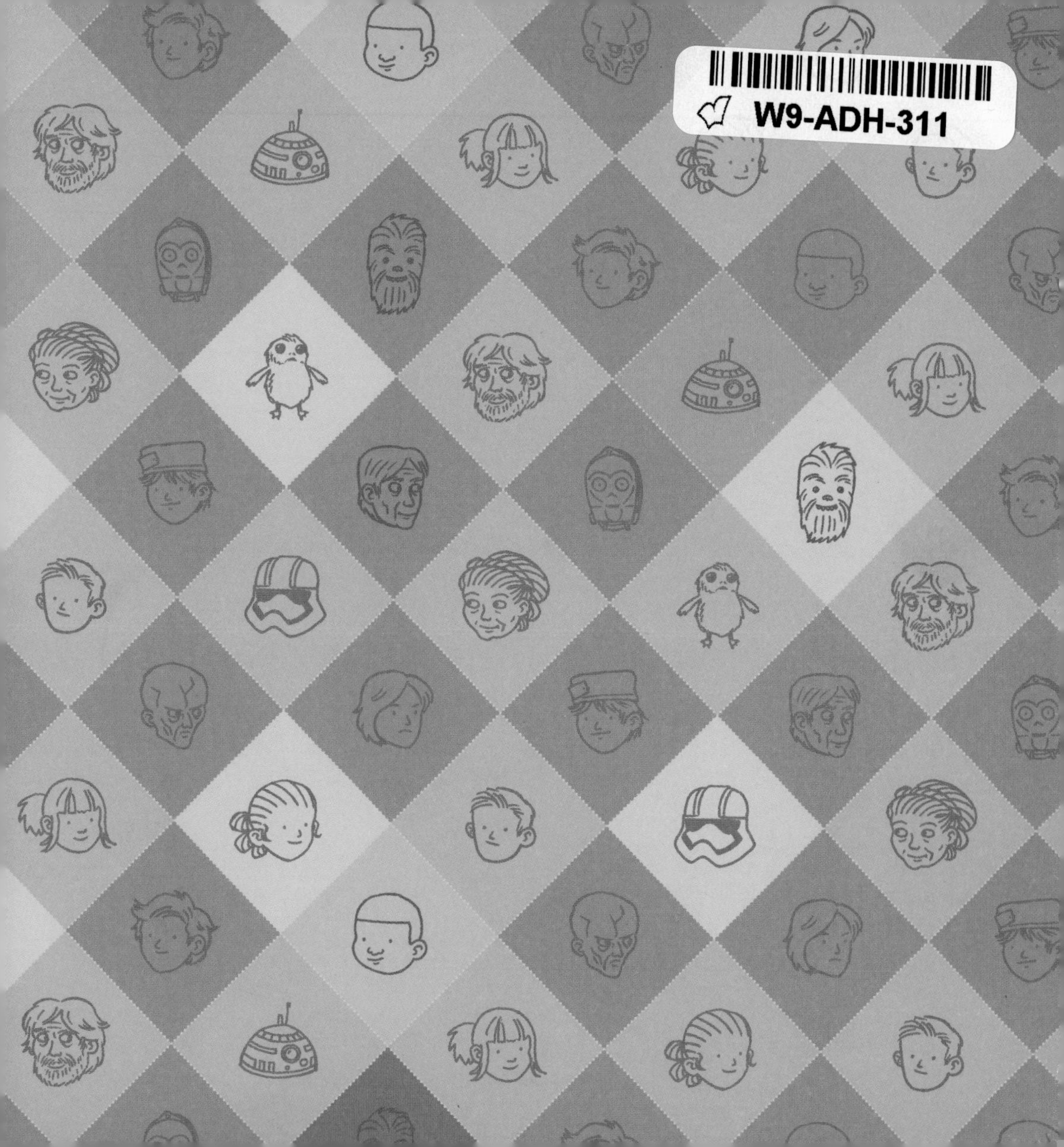

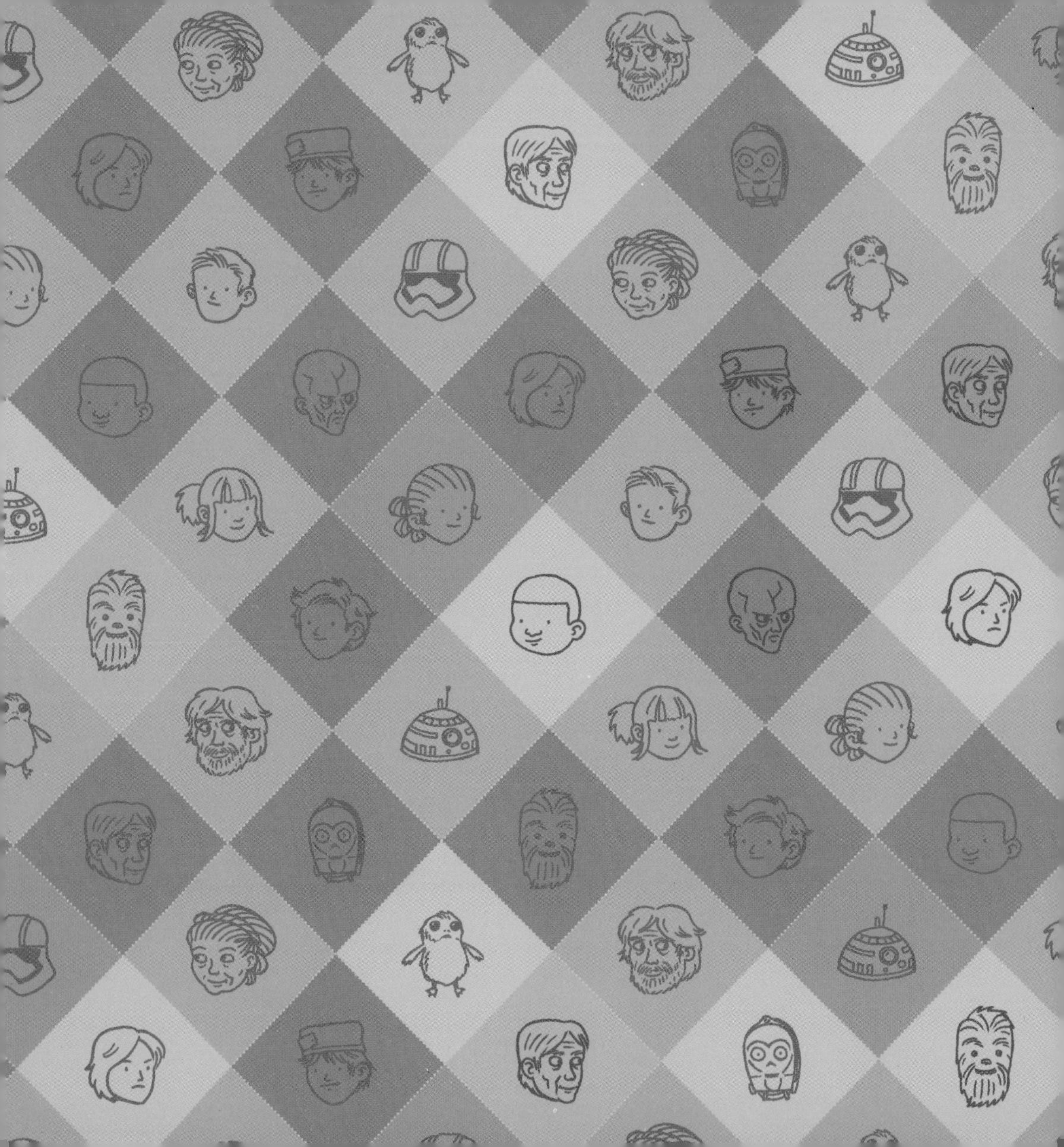

STAR WARS™
REY AND PALS

BY JEFFREY BROWN

CHRONICLE BOOKS
SAN FRANCISCO

LIBRARY OF CONGRESS CATALOGING-IN-PUBLICATION DATA IS AVAILABLE.

ISBN 978-1-4521-8043-4

MANUFACTURED IN CHINA.

MIX
Paper from responsible sources
FSC www.fsc.org
FSC™ C020056

WRITTEN AND DRAWN BY JEFFREY BROWN.
DESIGNED BY NEIL EGAN.

THANKS TO STEVE MOCKUS, J.W. RINZLER, MARC GERALD, MY FAMILY, AND ALL OF MY READERS. SPECIAL THANKS TO RYAN GERMICK AND MICHEAL LOPEZ AT GOOGLE FOR THE ORIGINAL INSPIRATION TO MAKE *DARTH VADER AND SON*.

10 9 8 7 6 5 4 3 2 1

CHRONICLE BOOKS LLC
680 SECOND STREET
SAN FRANCISCO, CALIFORNIA 94107

WWW.CHRONICLEBOOKS.COM

WWW.STARWARS.COM

A long time ago in a galaxy far, far away....

Episode High-Five:

REY AND PALS

Luke Skywalker is all grown up, and the FIRST ORDER has risen from the ashes of the Empire. But there's a new generation of RESISTANCE, and they will not rest until they restore FUN to the galaxy....

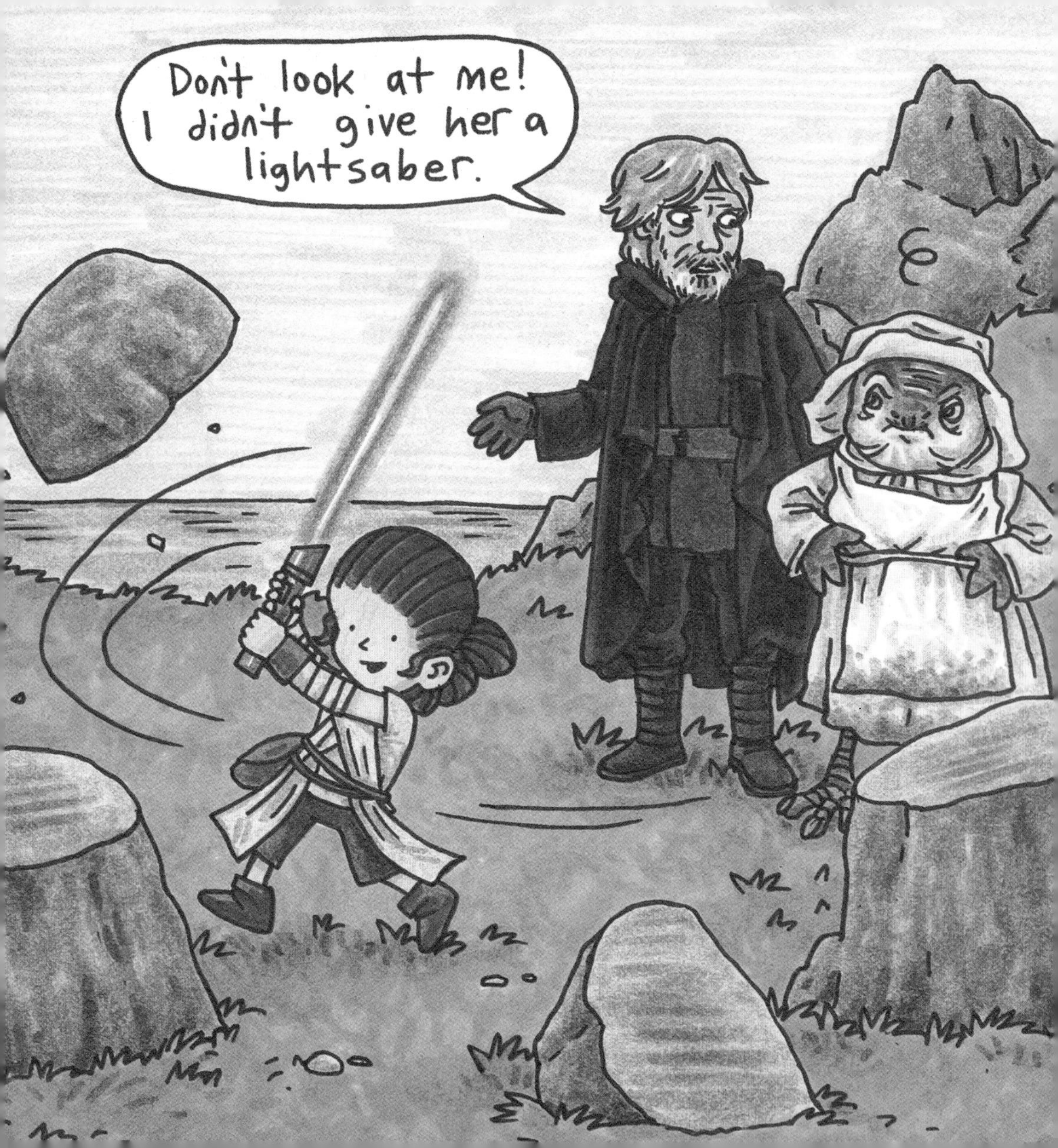
Don't look at me! I didn't give her a lightsaber.

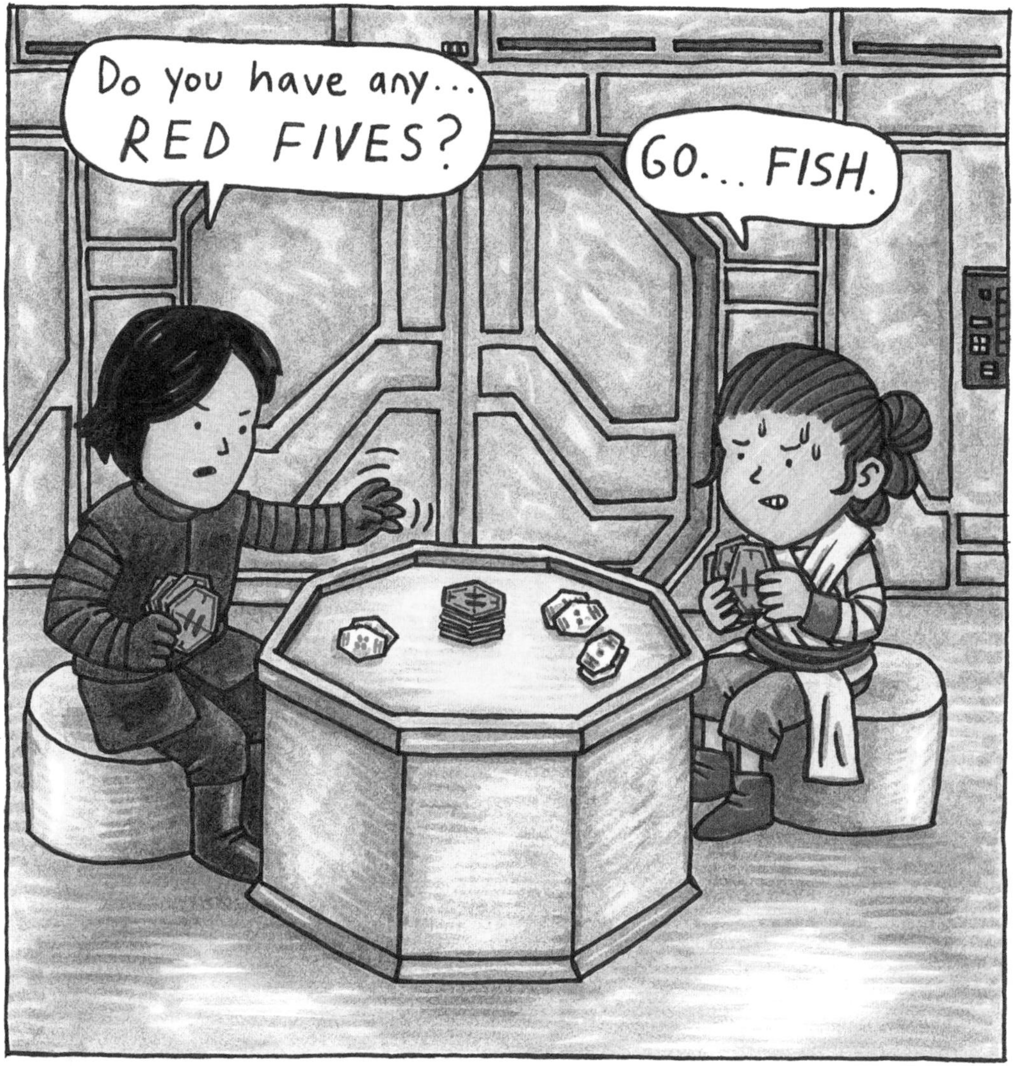
Do you have any...
RED FIVES?
GO... FISH.

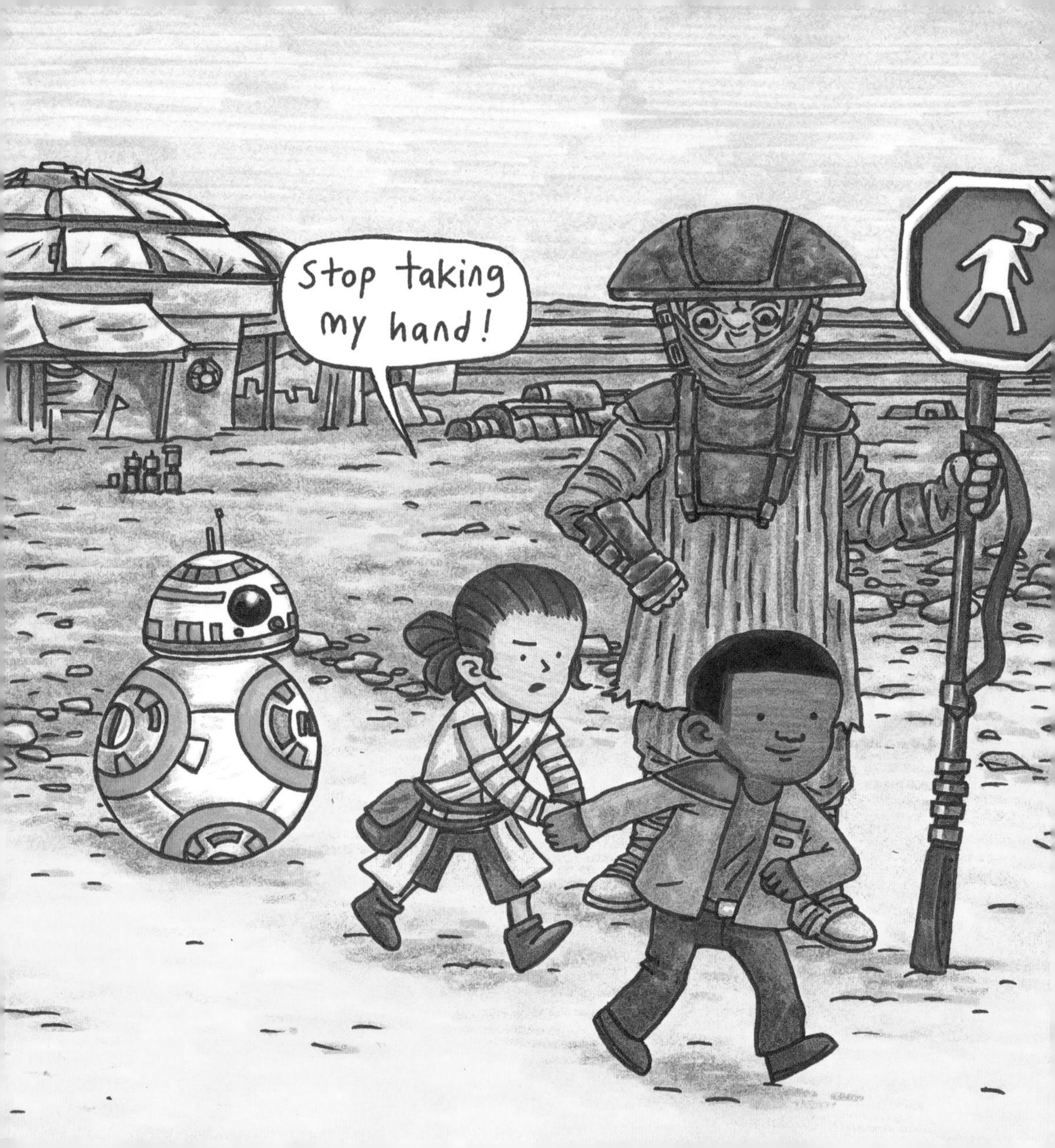
Stop taking my hand!

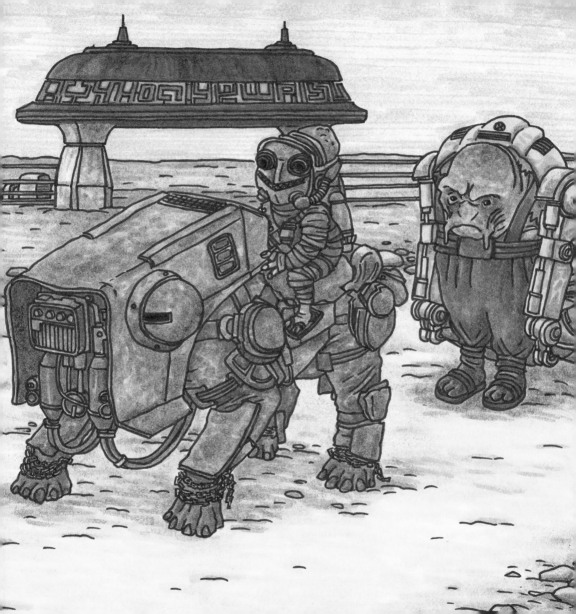

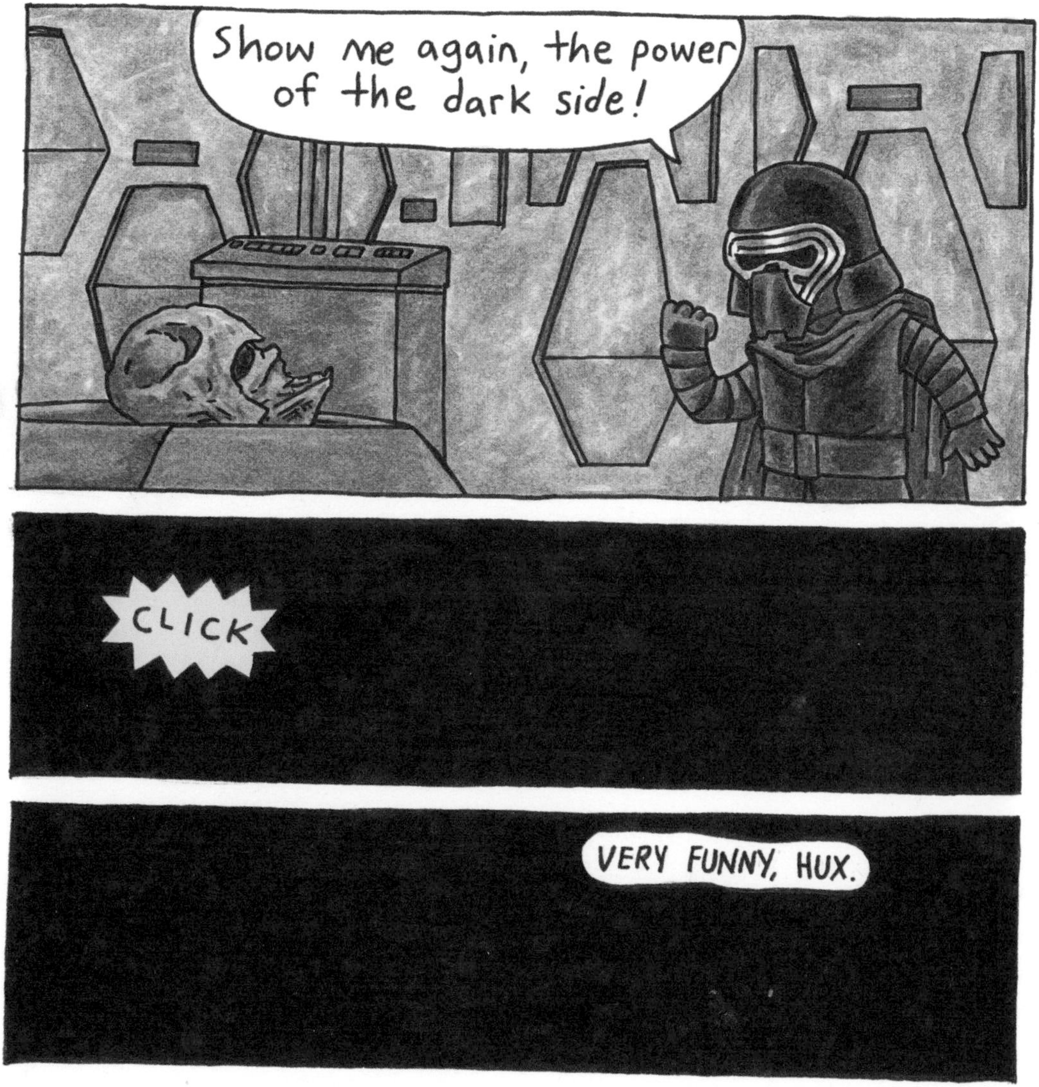
Show me again, the power of the dark side!
CLICK
VERY FUNNY, HUX.

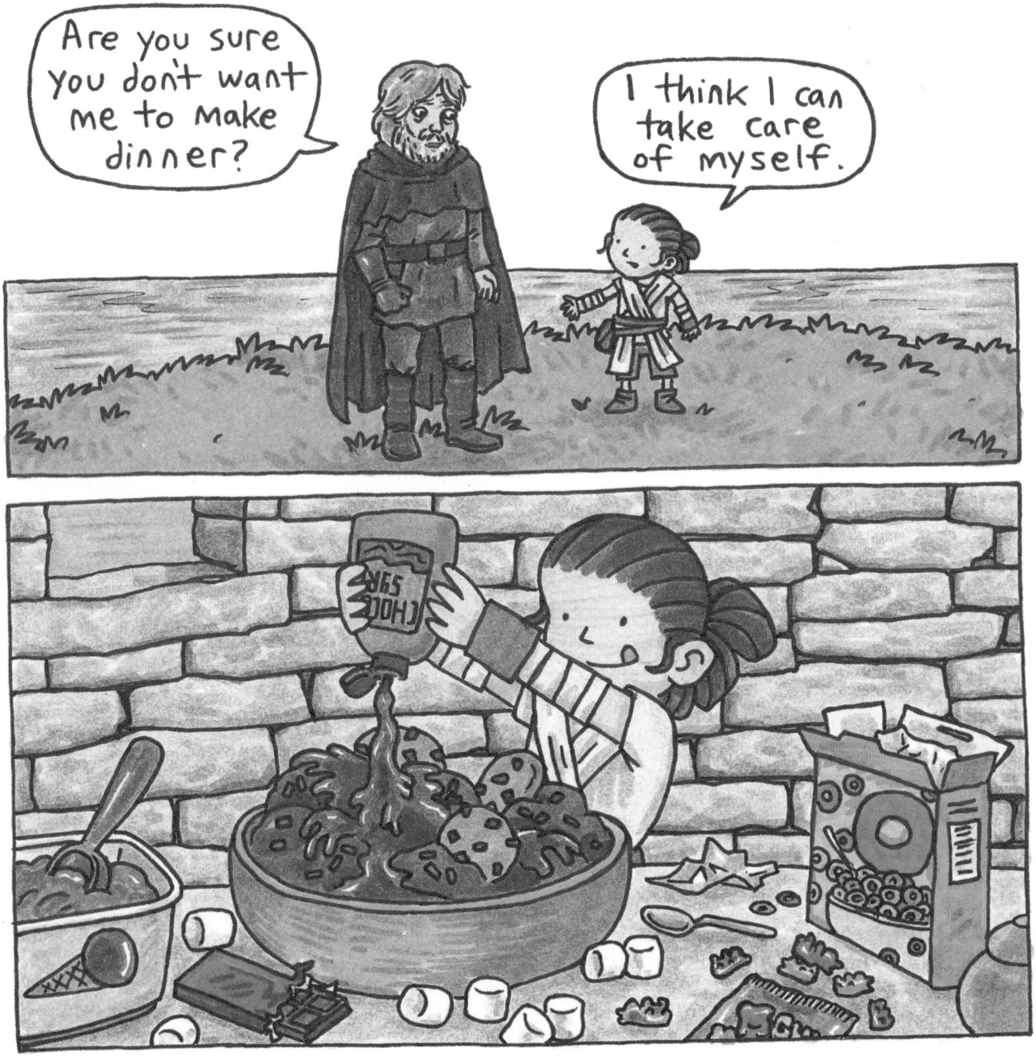
Are you sure you don't want me to make dinner?
I think I can take care of myself.

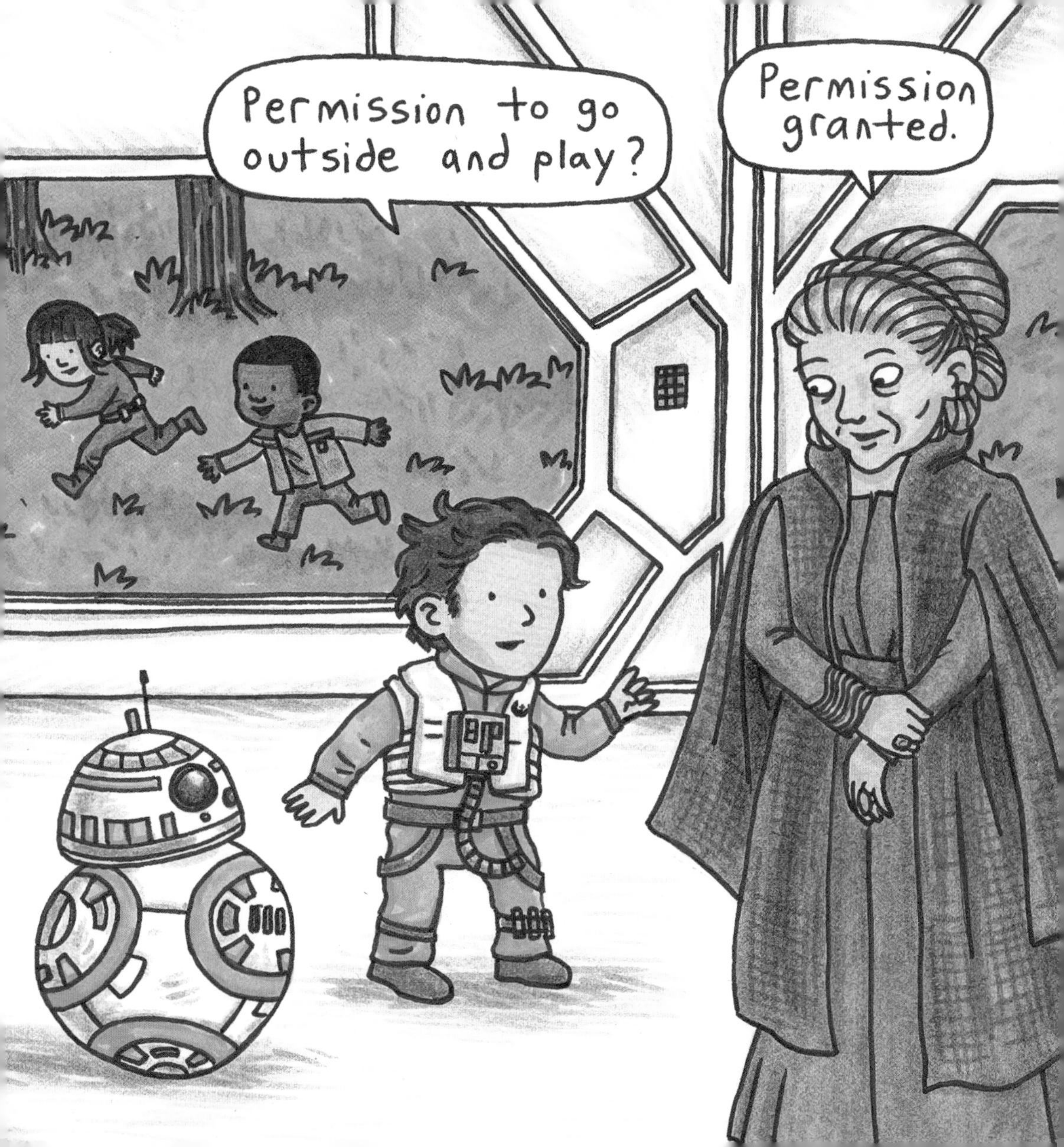
Permission to go outside and play?
Permission granted.

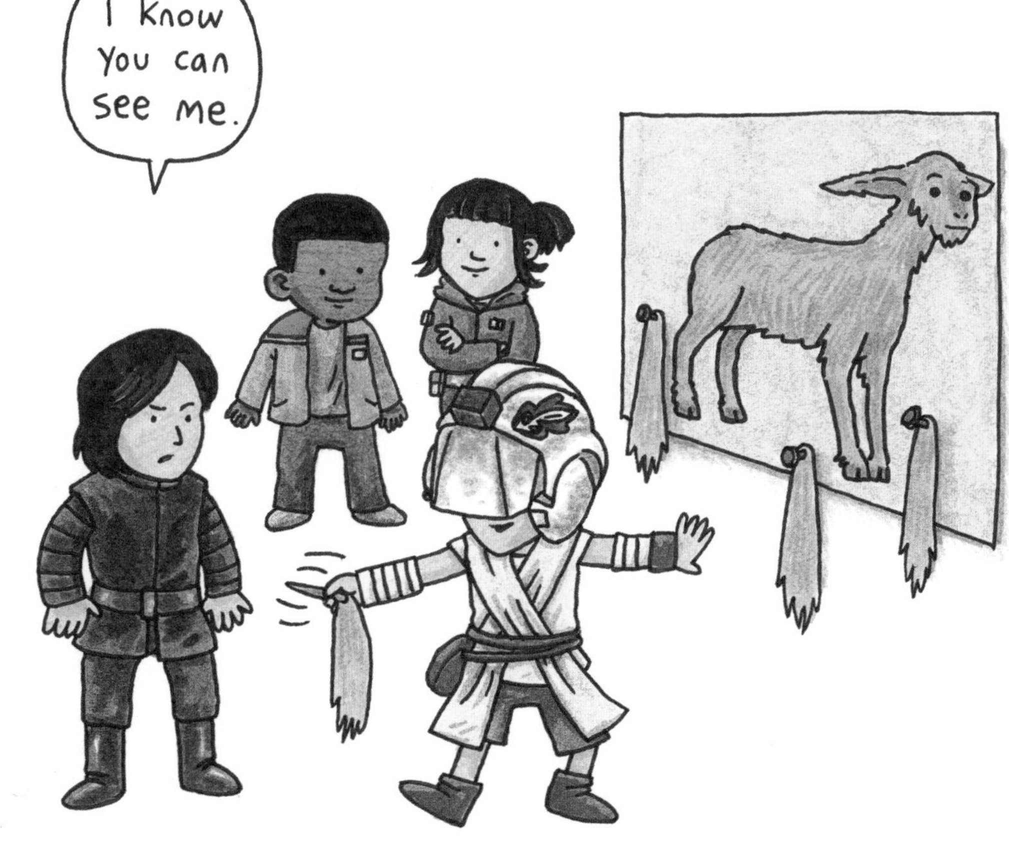
I know you can see me.

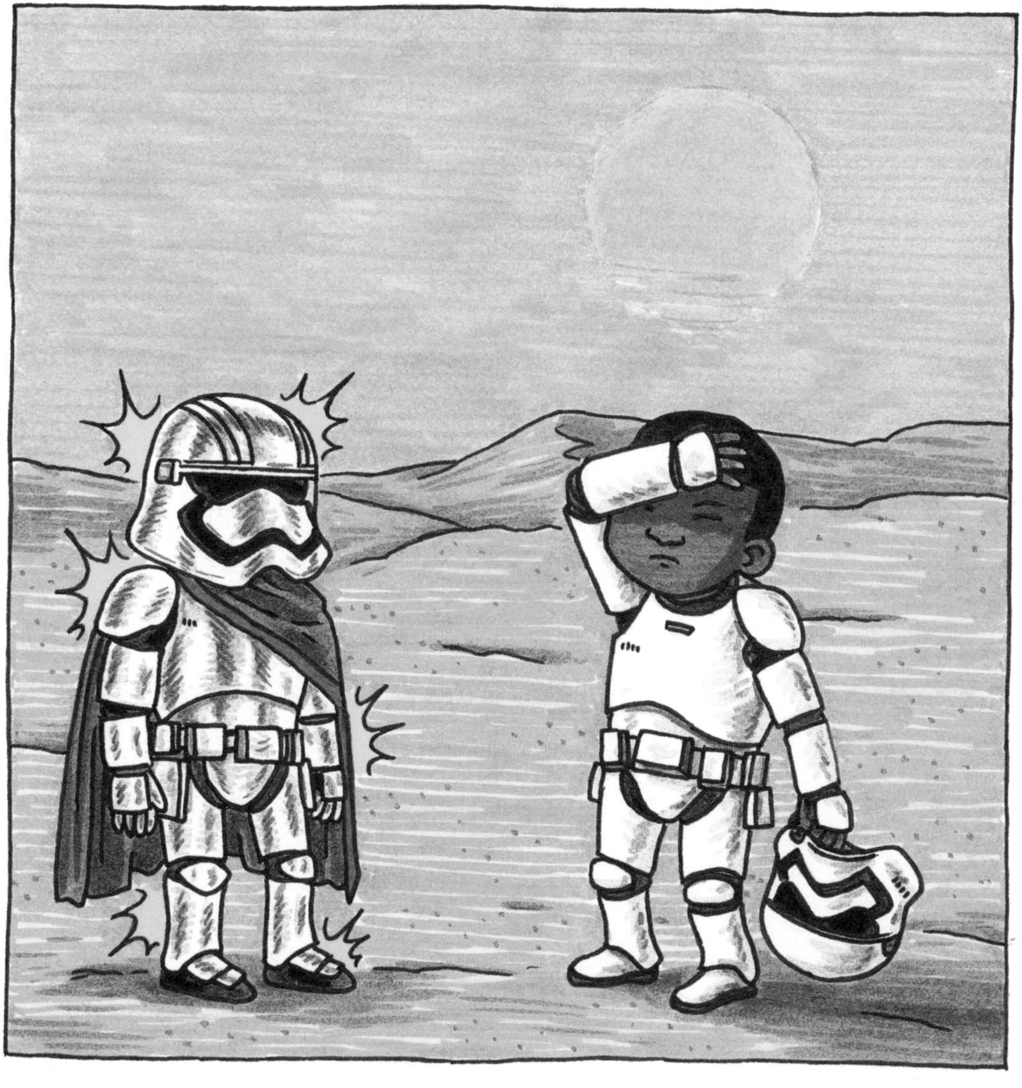

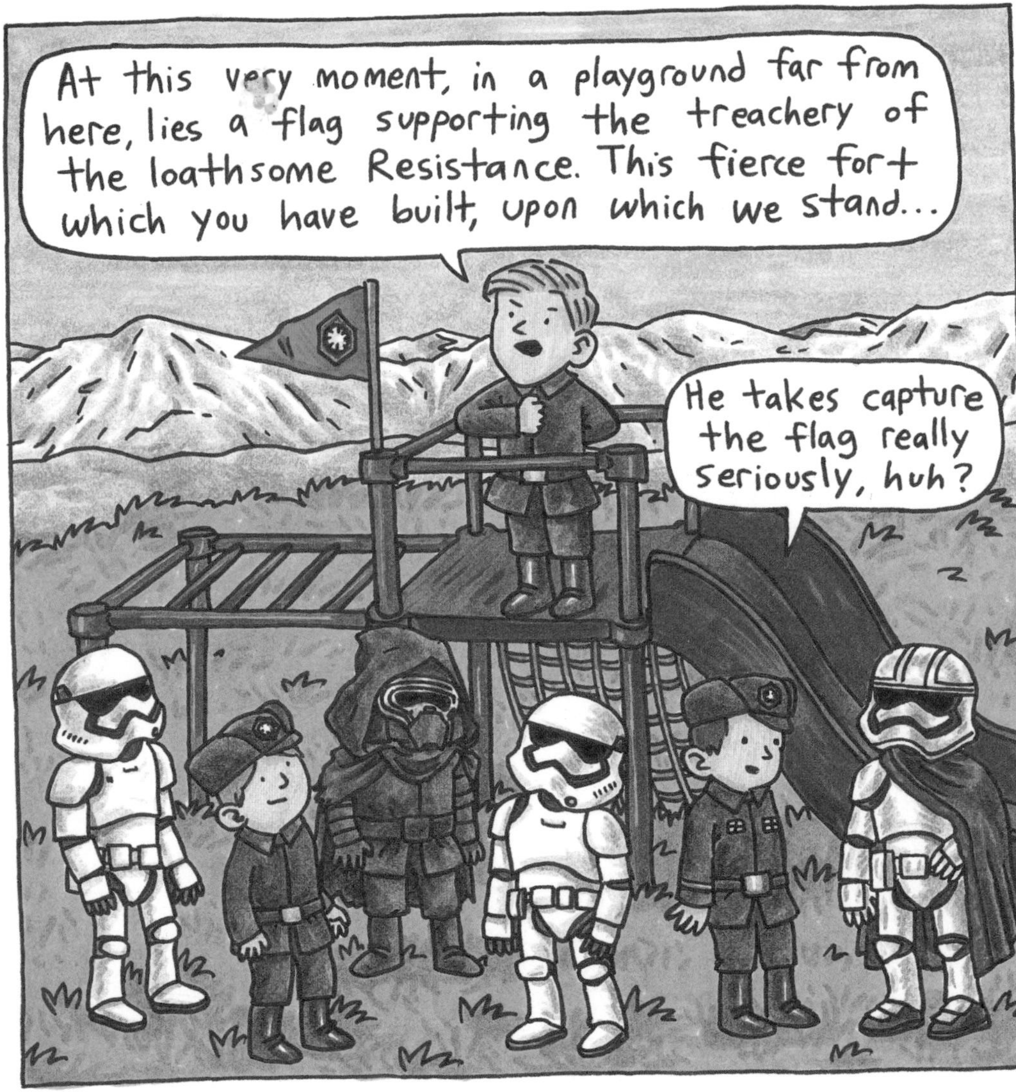
At this very moment, in a playground far from here, lies a flag supporting the treachery of the loathsome Resistance. This fierce fort which you have built, upon which we stand...
He takes capture the flag really seriously, huh?

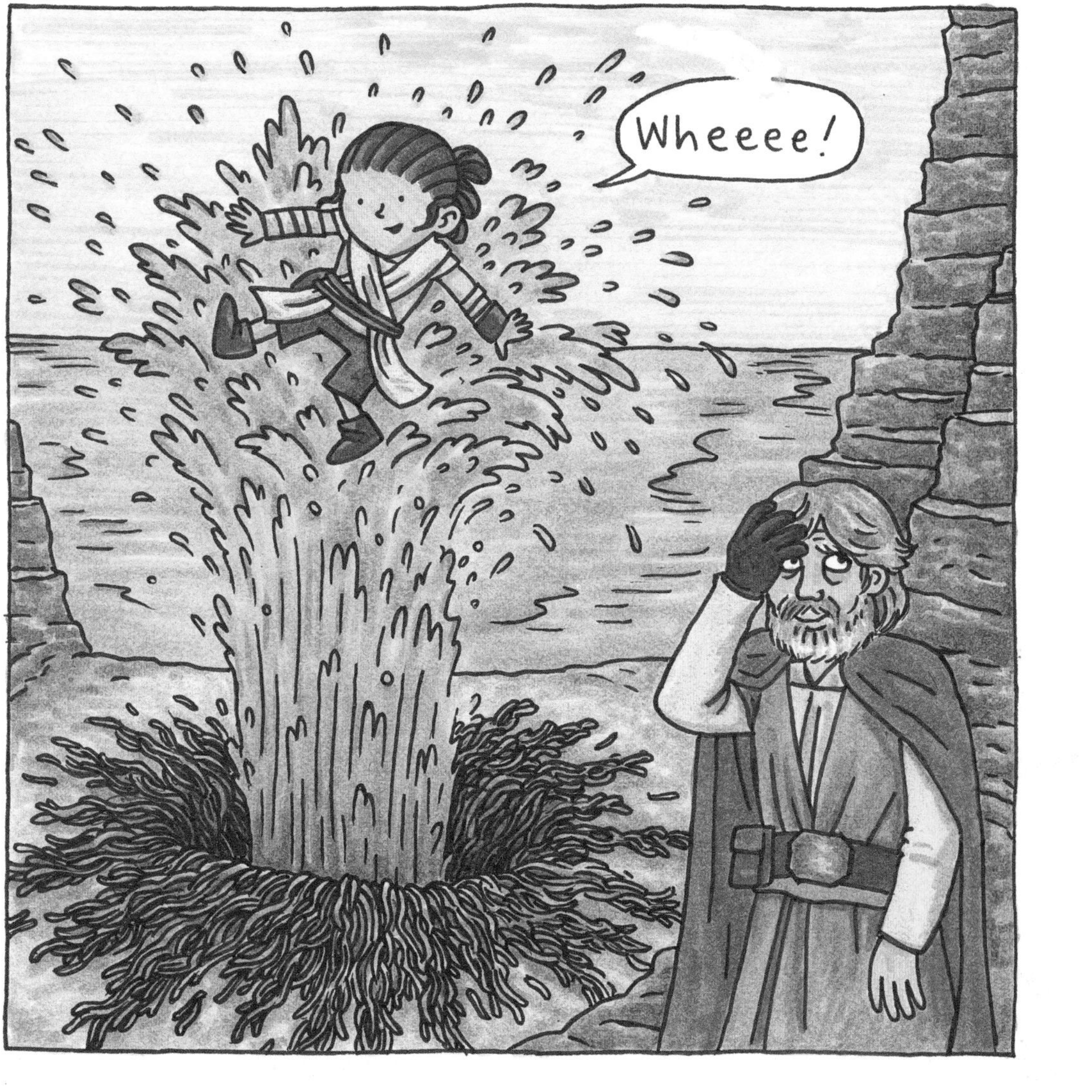
Wheeee!

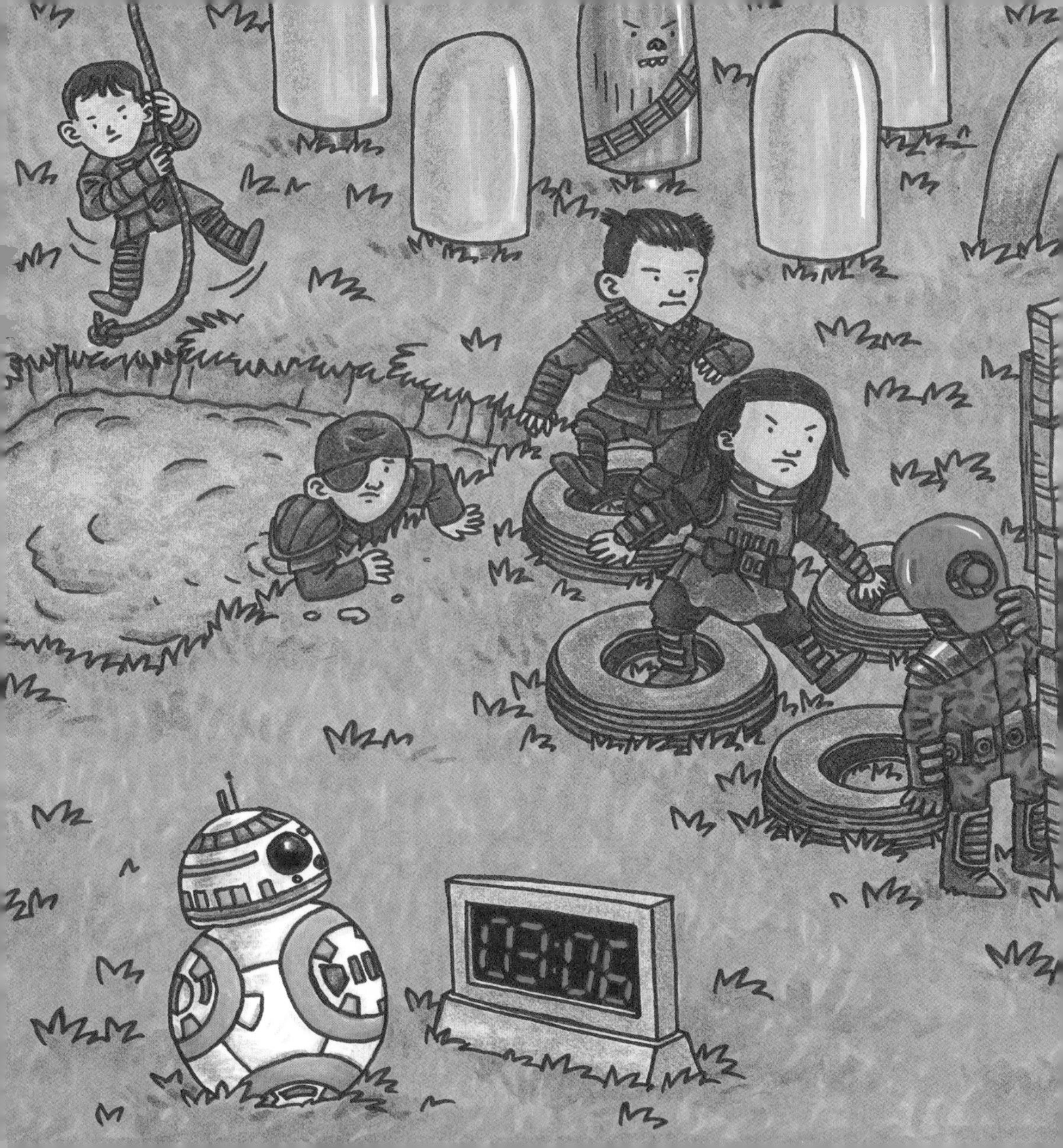

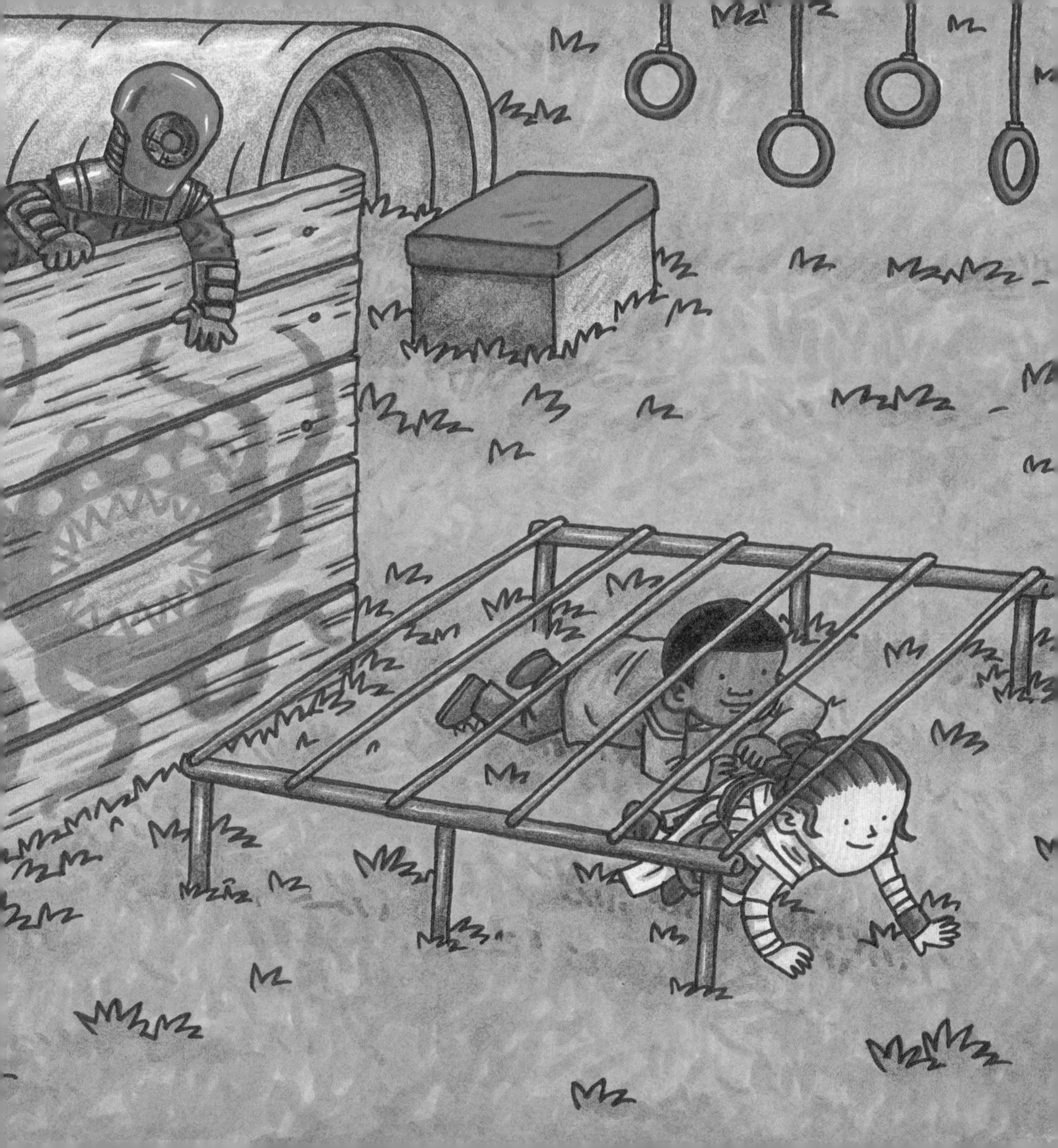

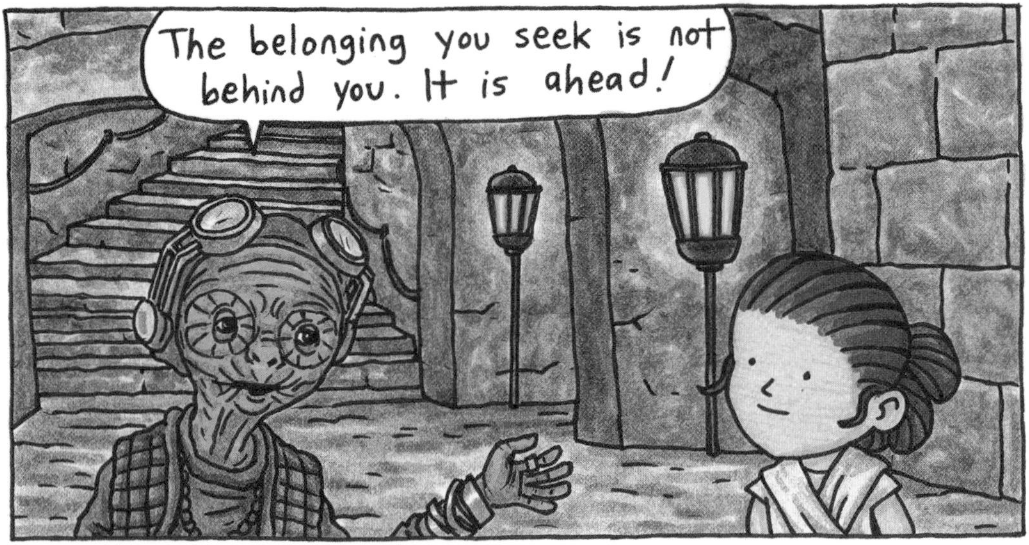
The belonging you seek is not behind you. It is ahead!

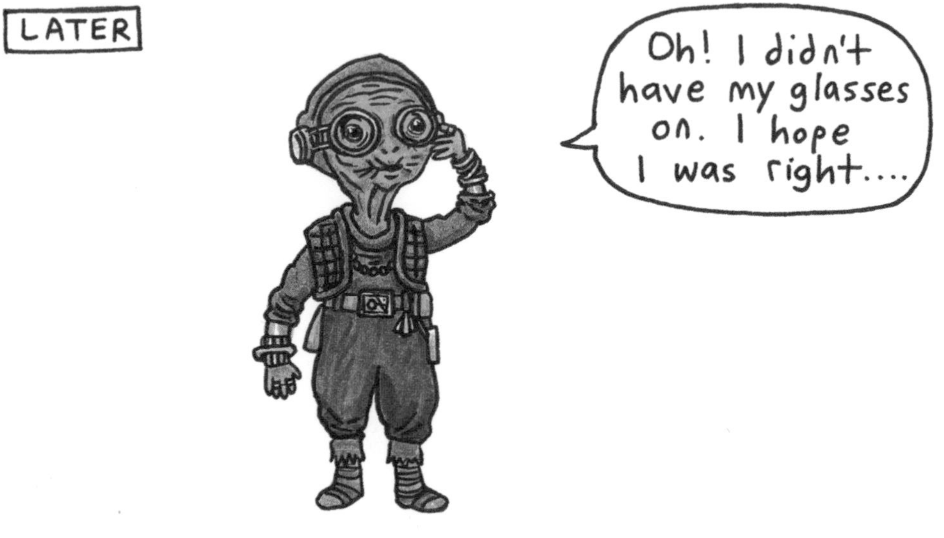
LATER
Oh! I didn't have my glasses on. I hope I was right....

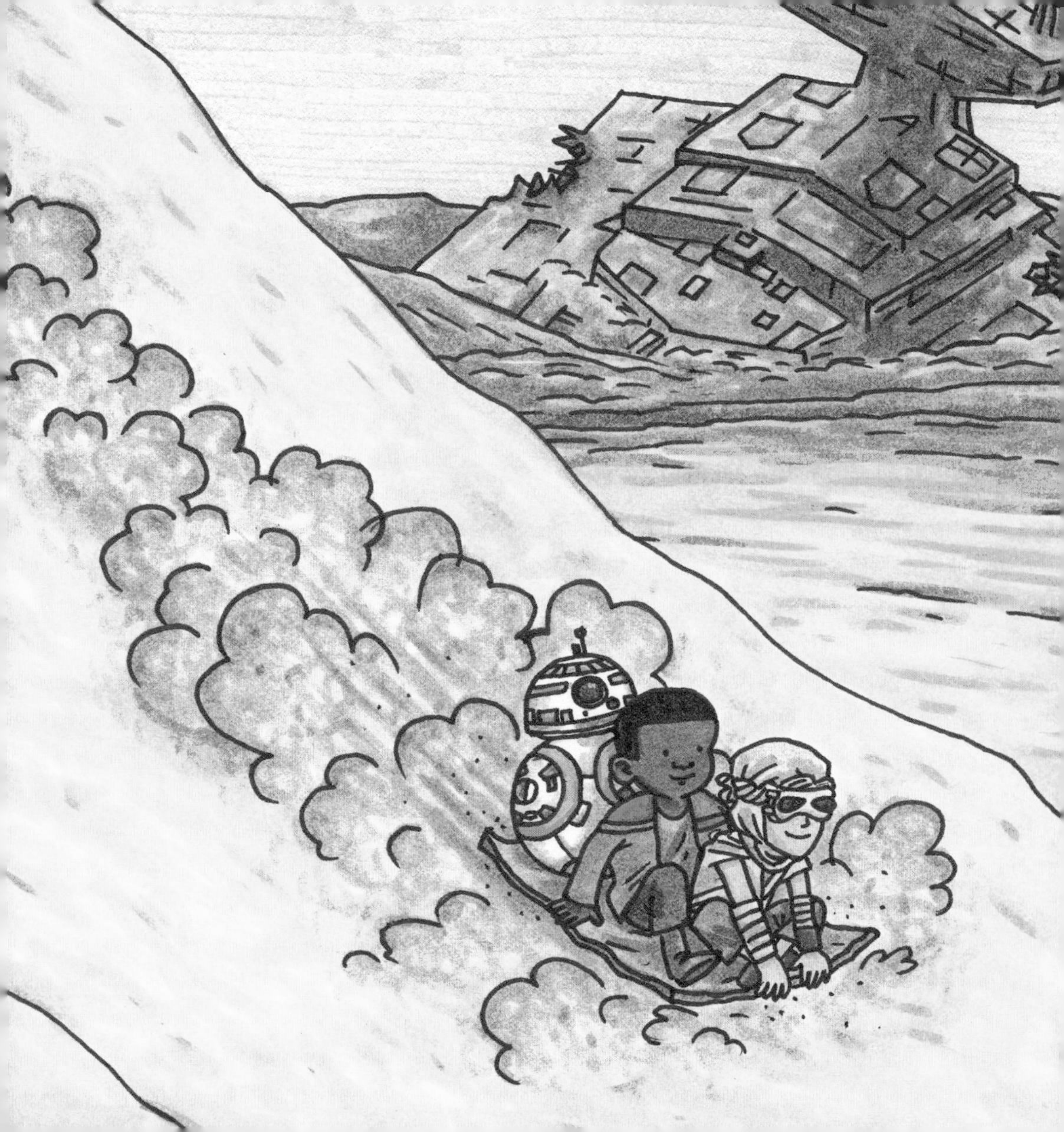

I'm not sure you want to let Master Luke see you in that costume, BB-8.

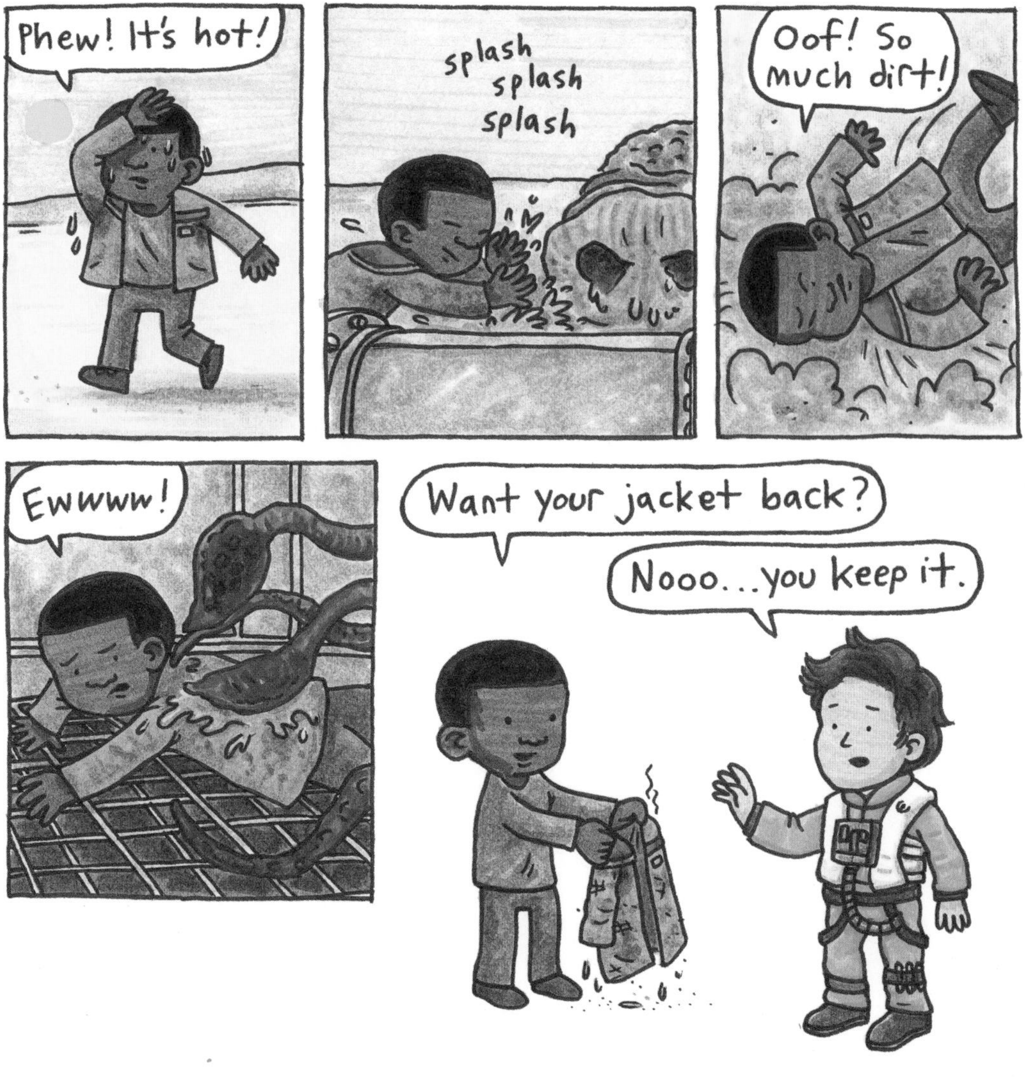
Phew! It's hot!
splash
splash
splash
Oof! So much dirt!
Ewwww!
Want your jacket back?
Nooo...you keep it.

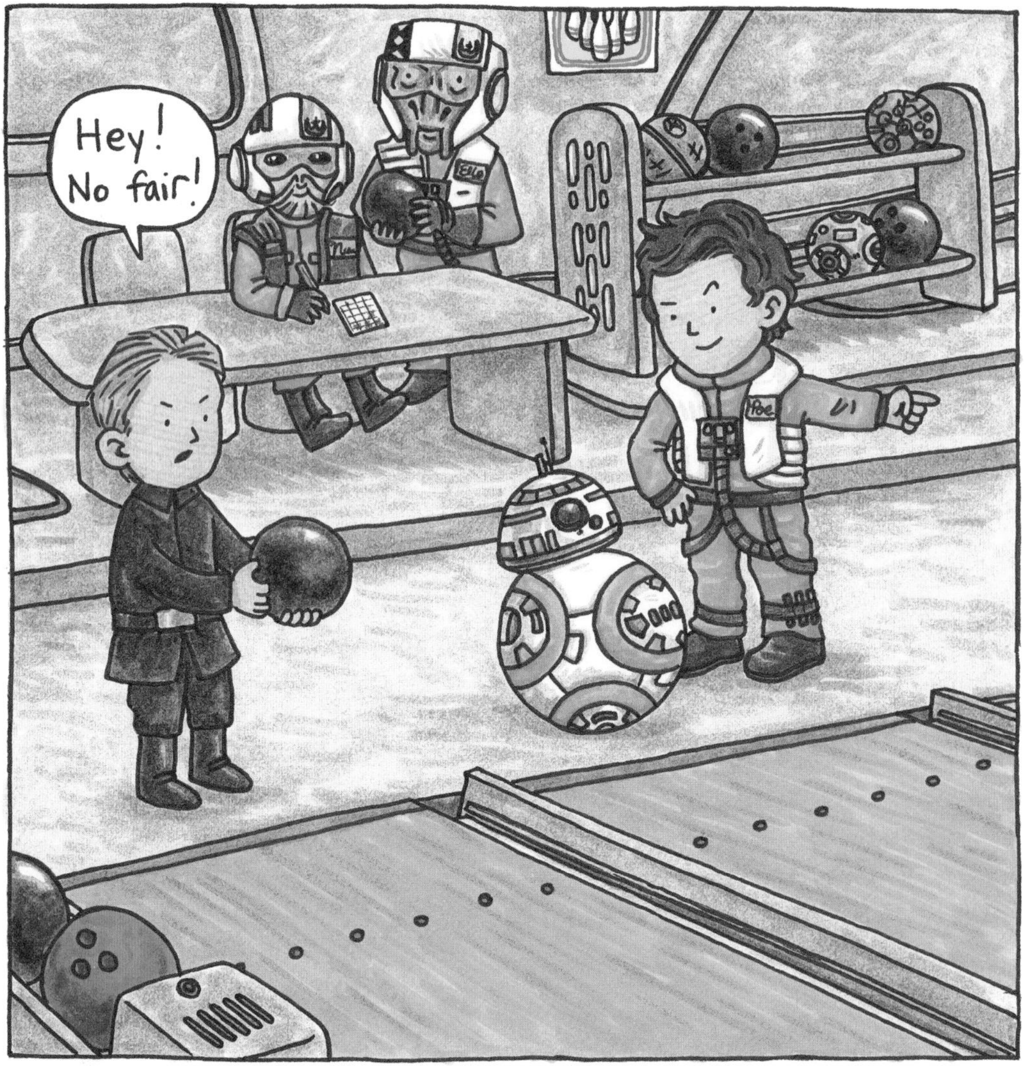
Hey! No fair!

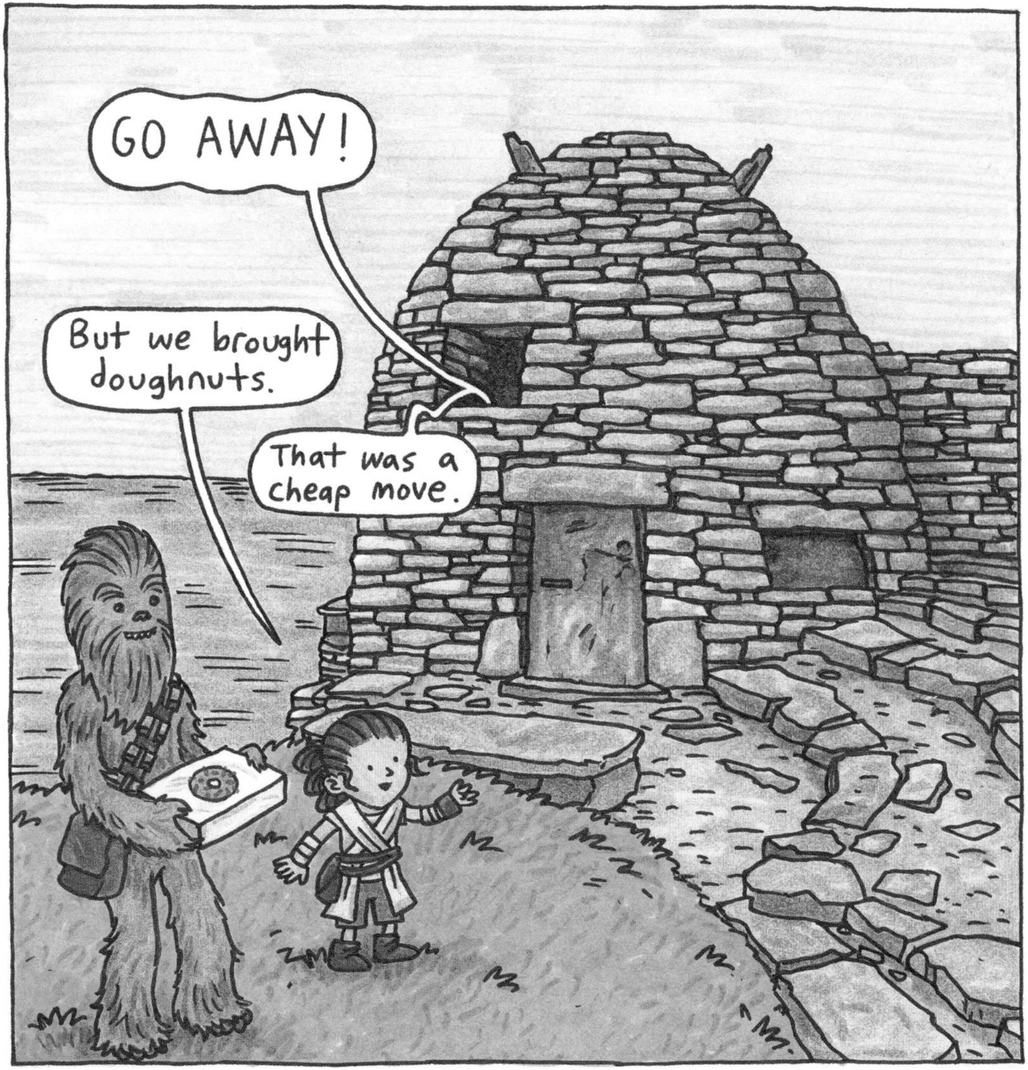
GO AWAY!
But we brought doughnuts.
That was a cheap move.

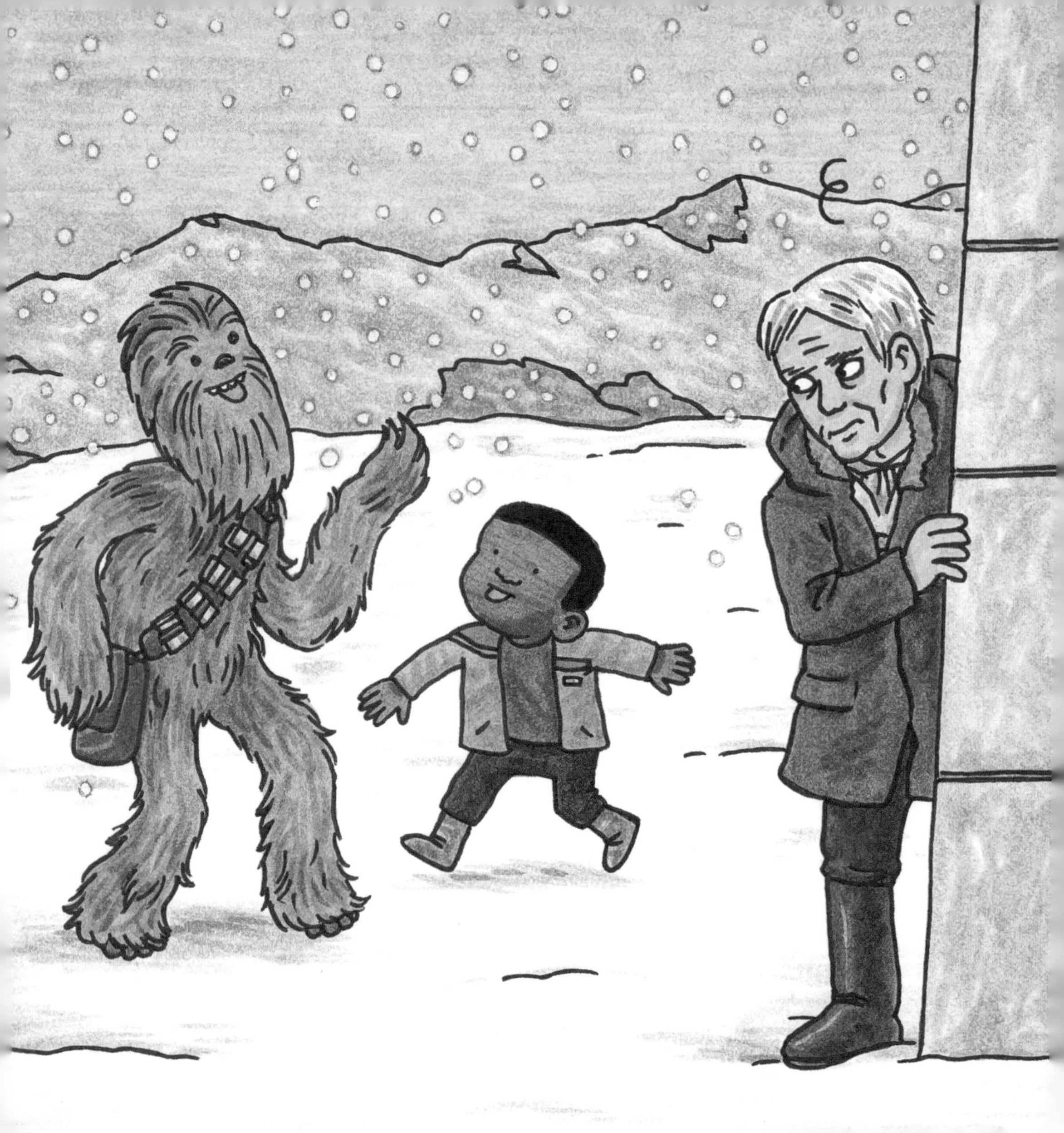

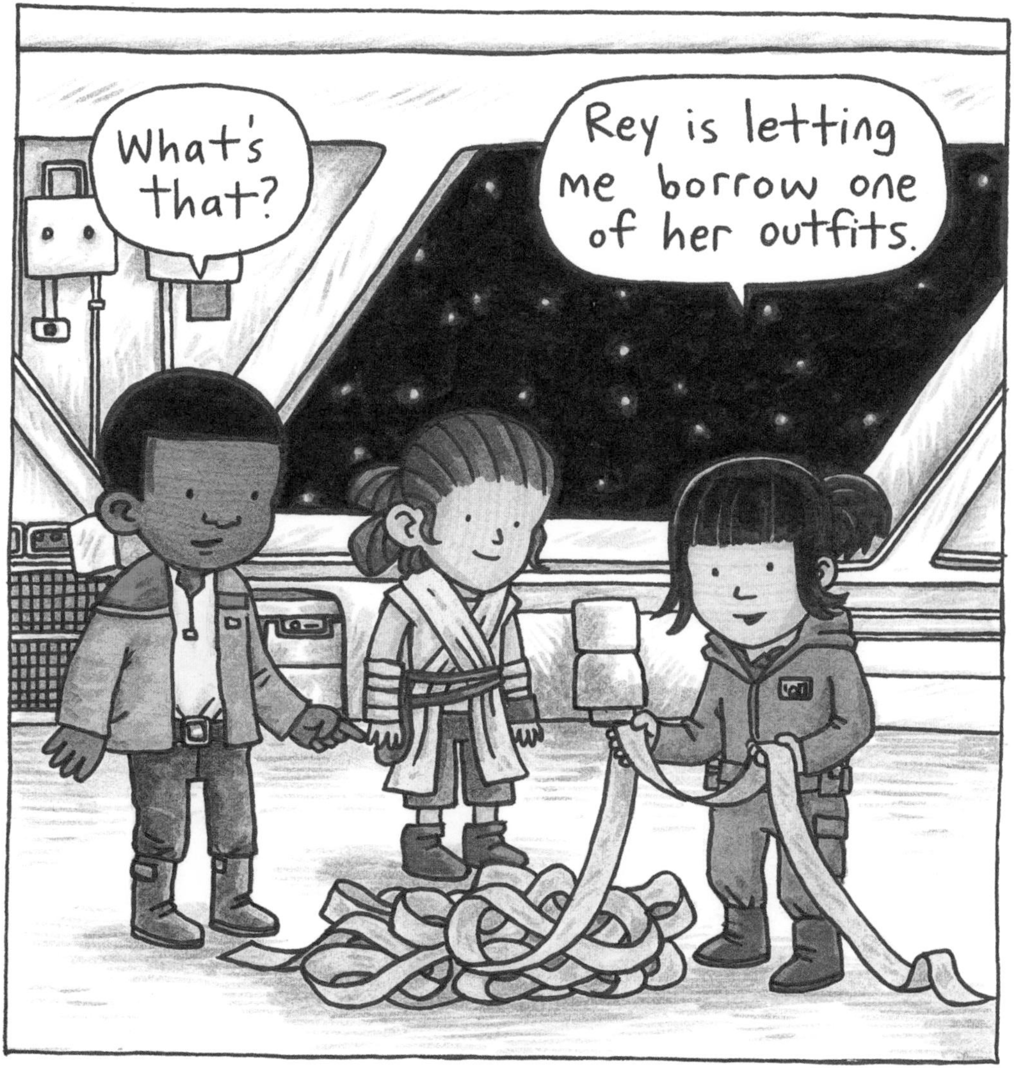
What's that?
Rey is letting me borrow one of her outfits.

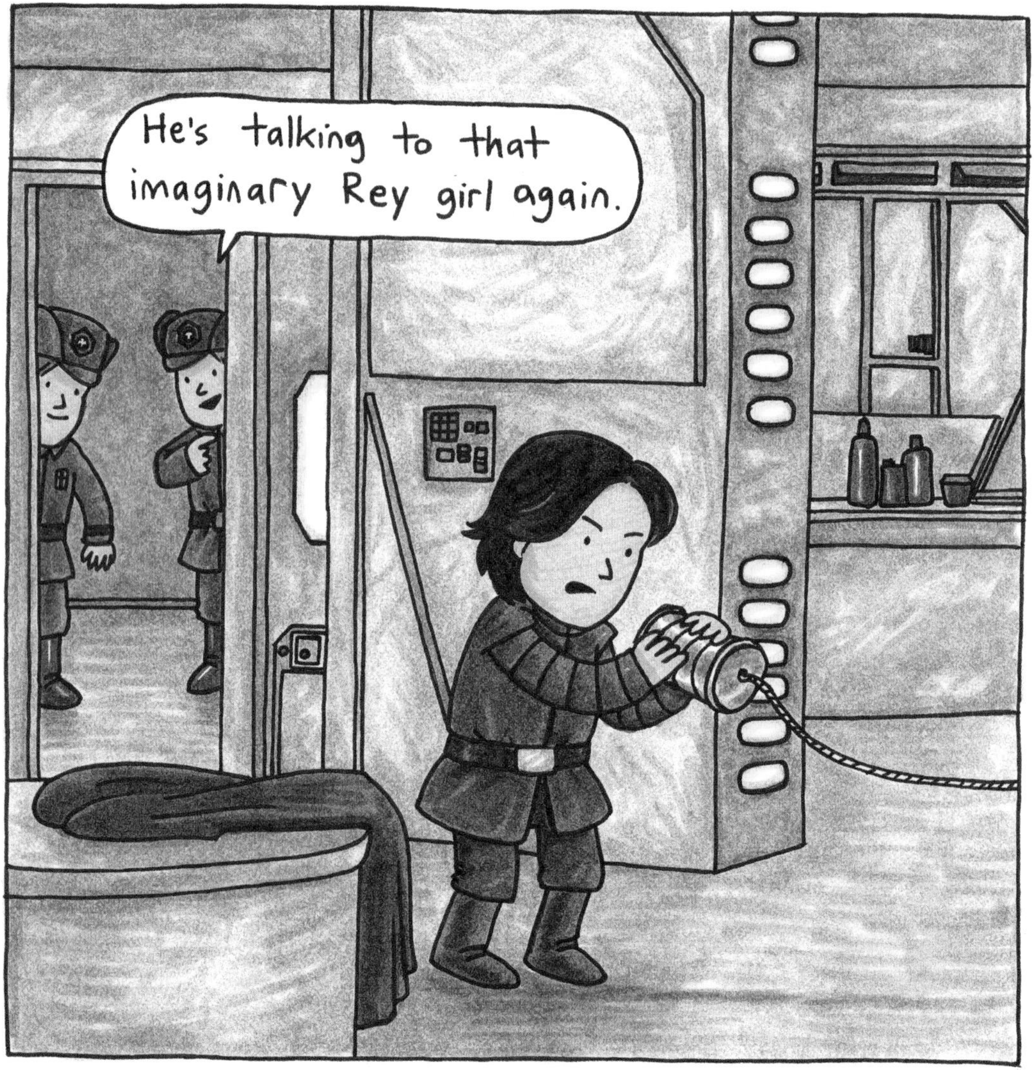
He's talking to that imaginary Rey girl again.

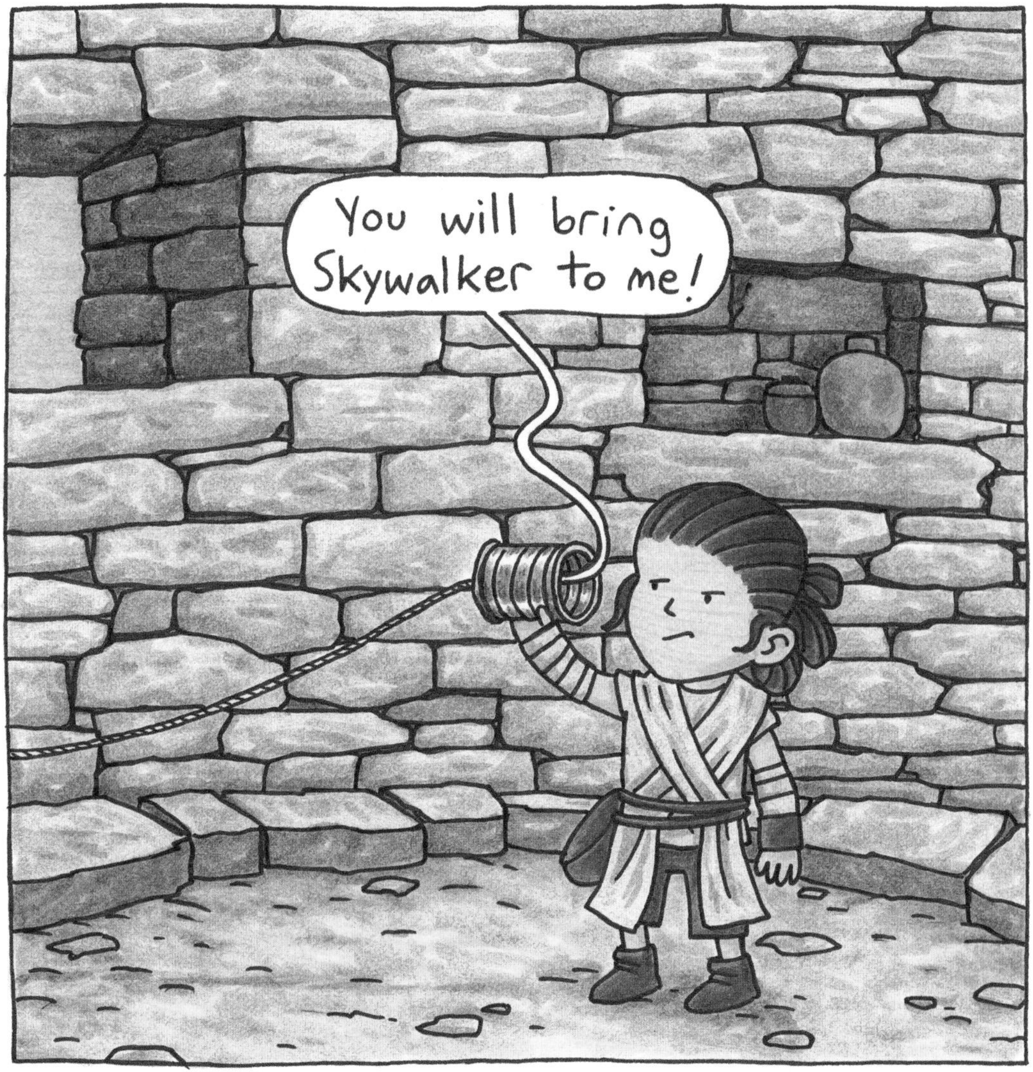
You will bring Skywalker to me!

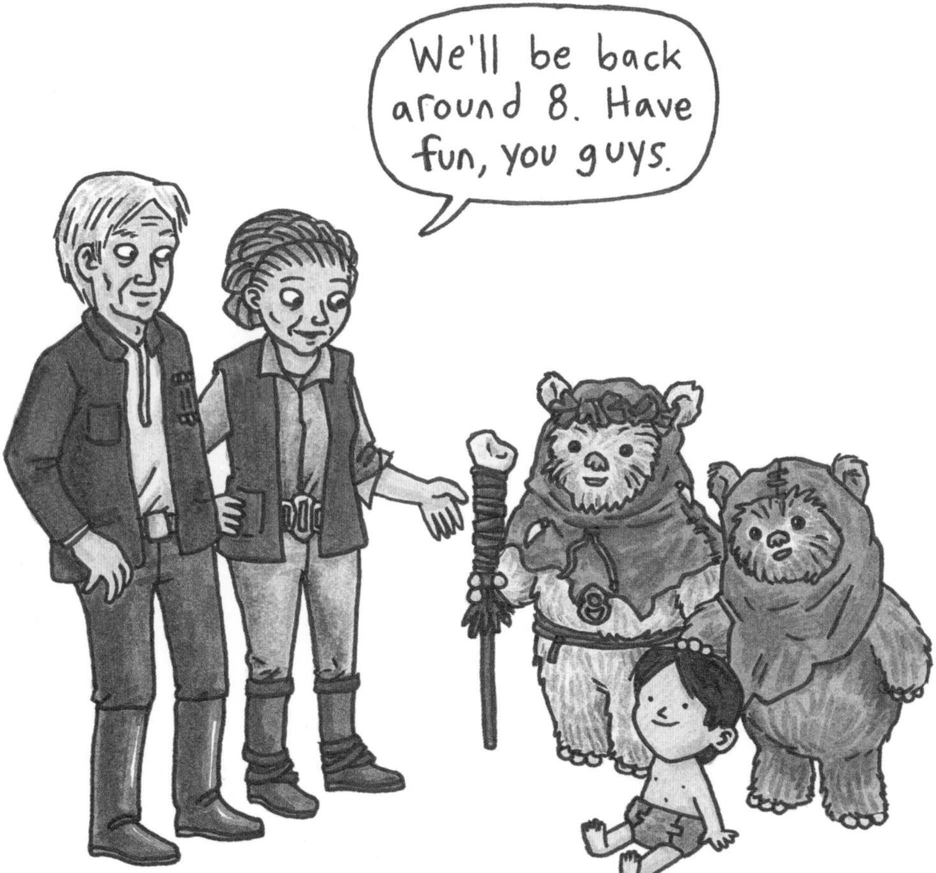
We'll be back around 8. Have fun, you guys.

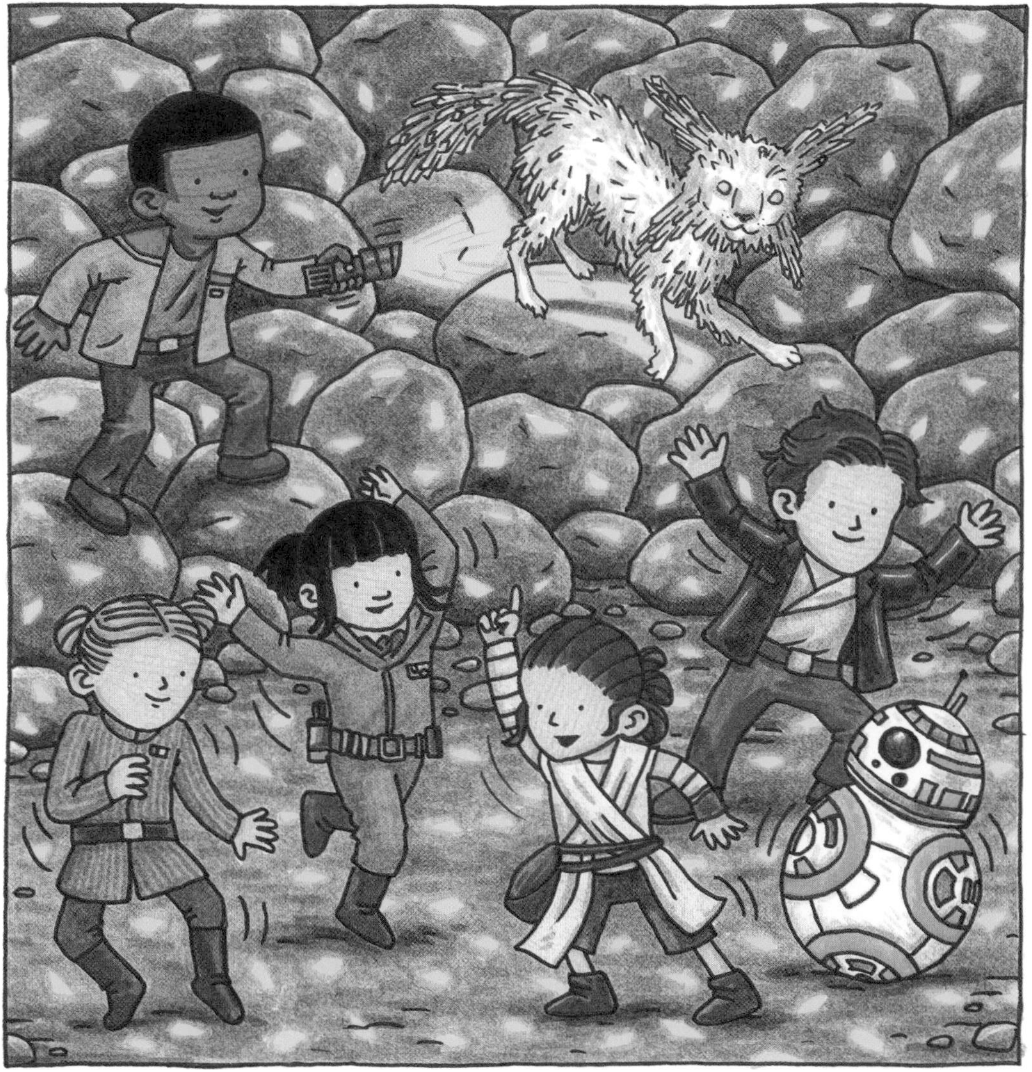

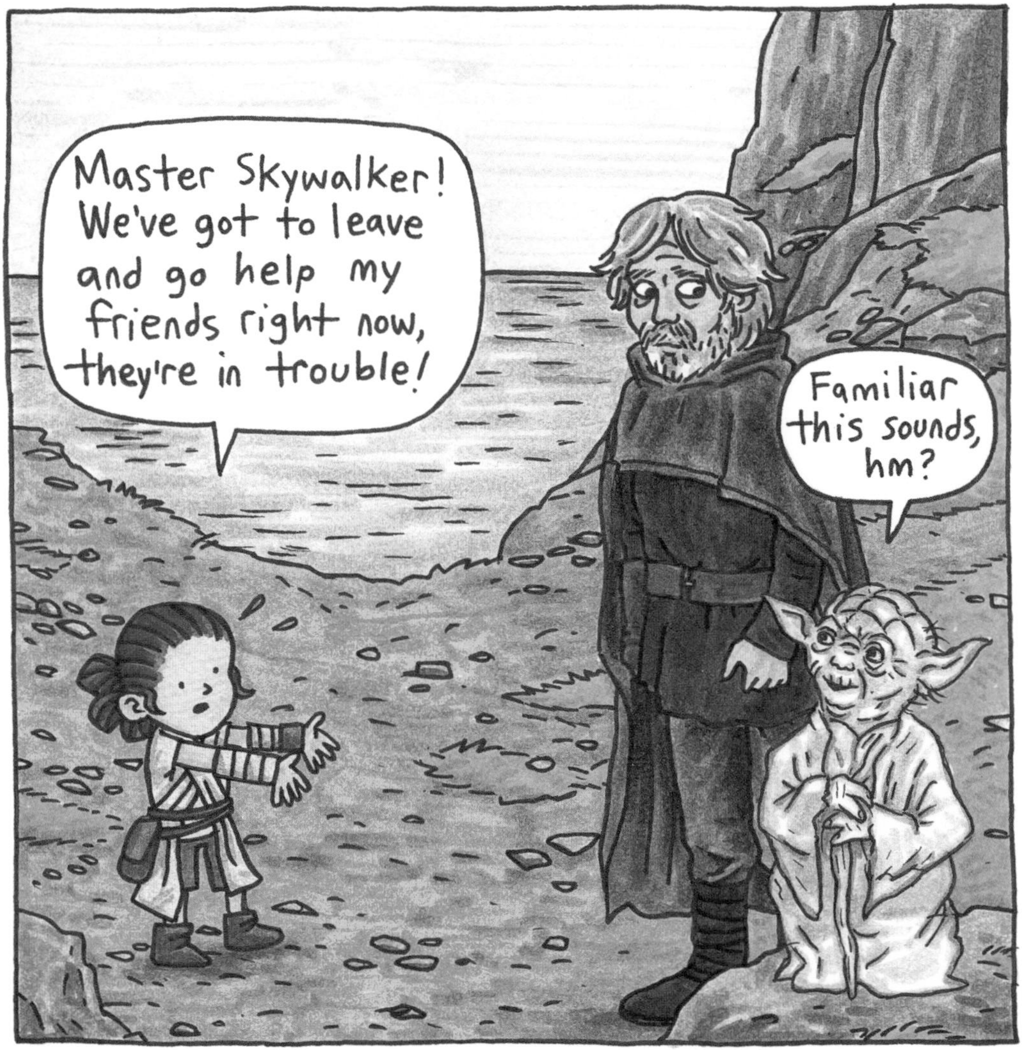
Master Skywalker! We've got to leave and go help my friends right now, they're in trouble!
Familiar this sounds, hm?

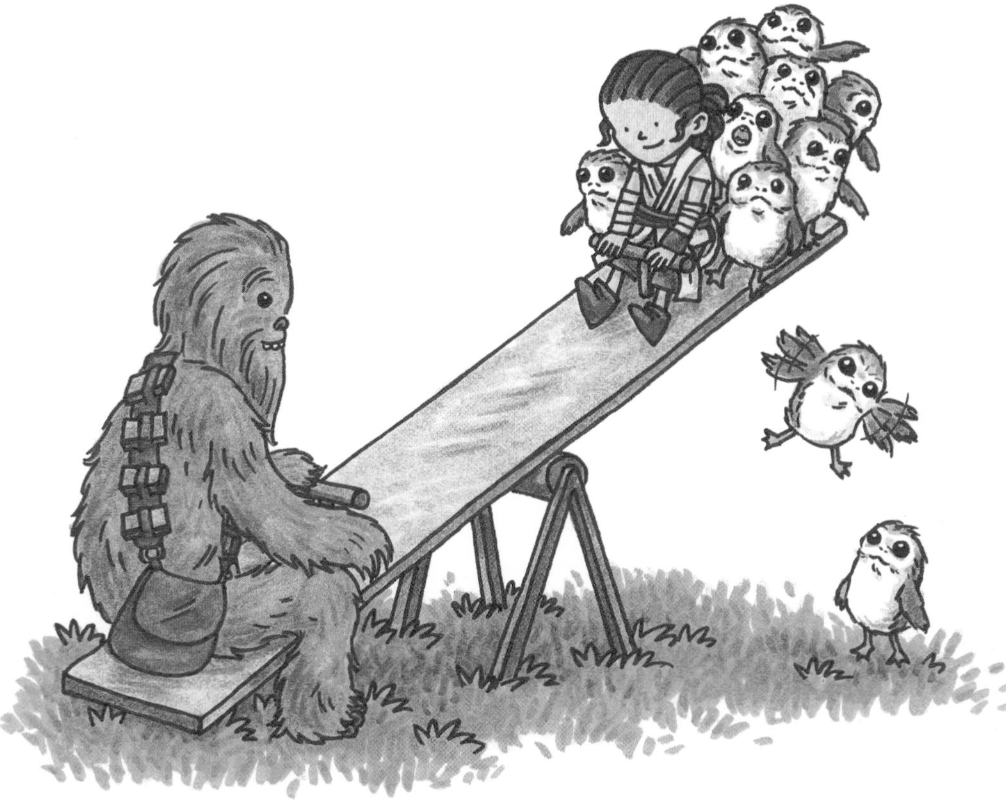

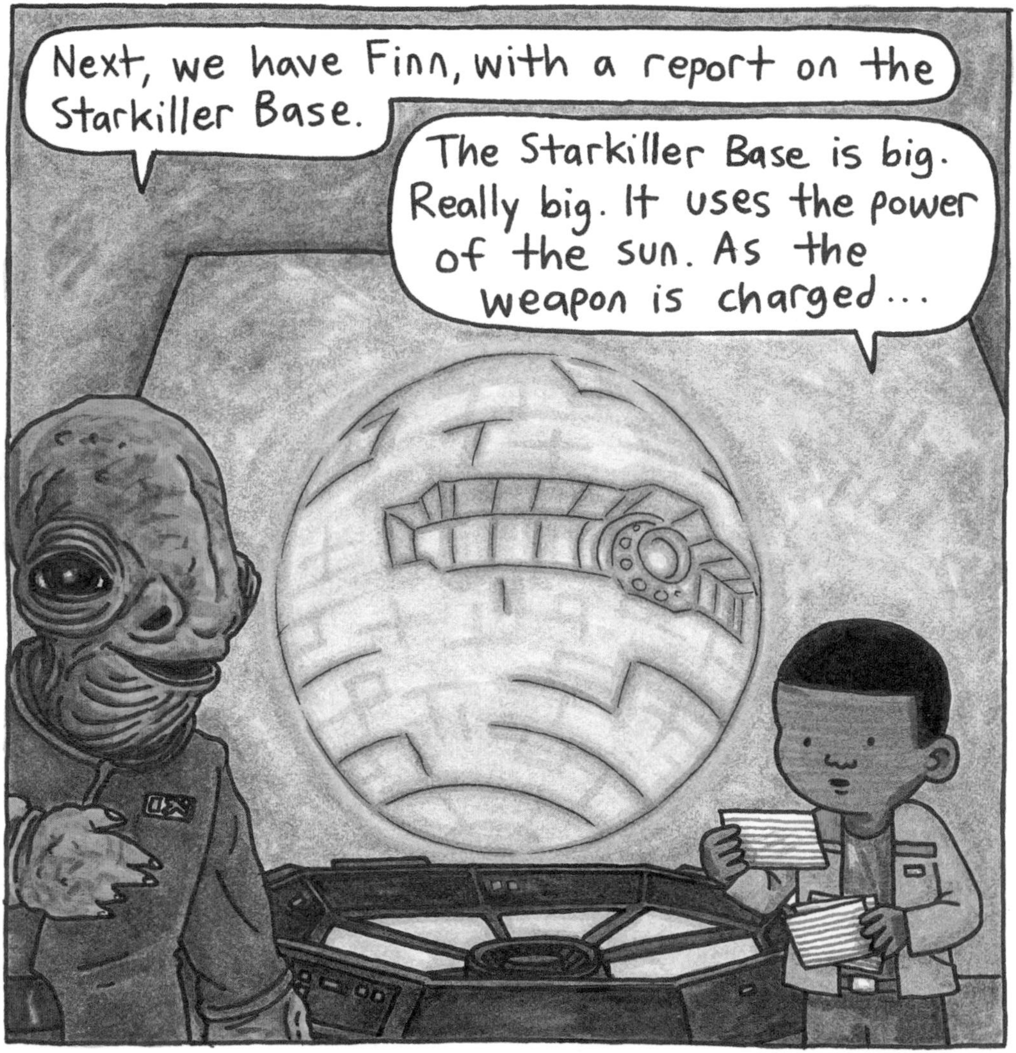
Next, we have Finn, with a report on the Starkiller Base.
The Starkiller Base is big. Really big. It uses the power of the sun. As the weapon is charged...

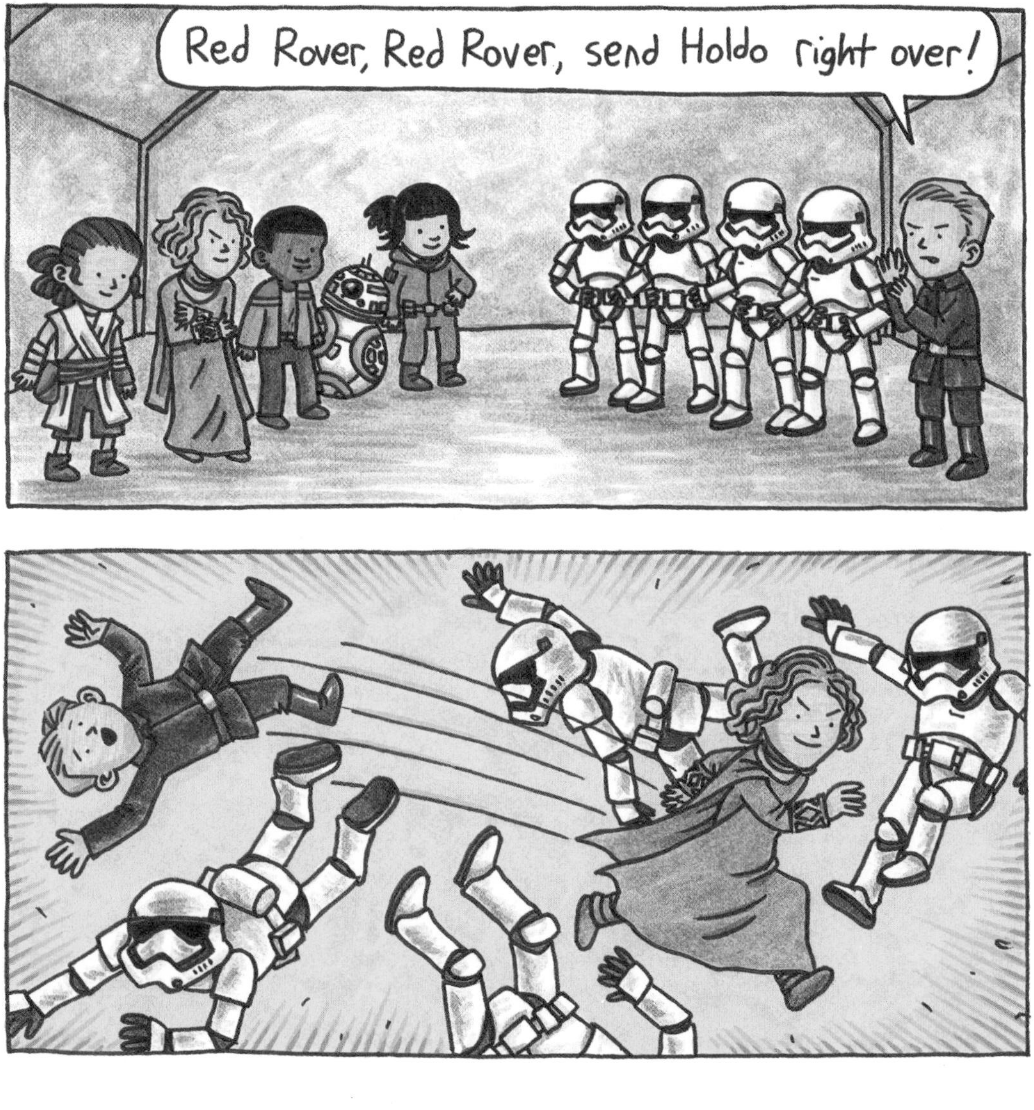
Red Rover, Red Rover, send Holdo right over!

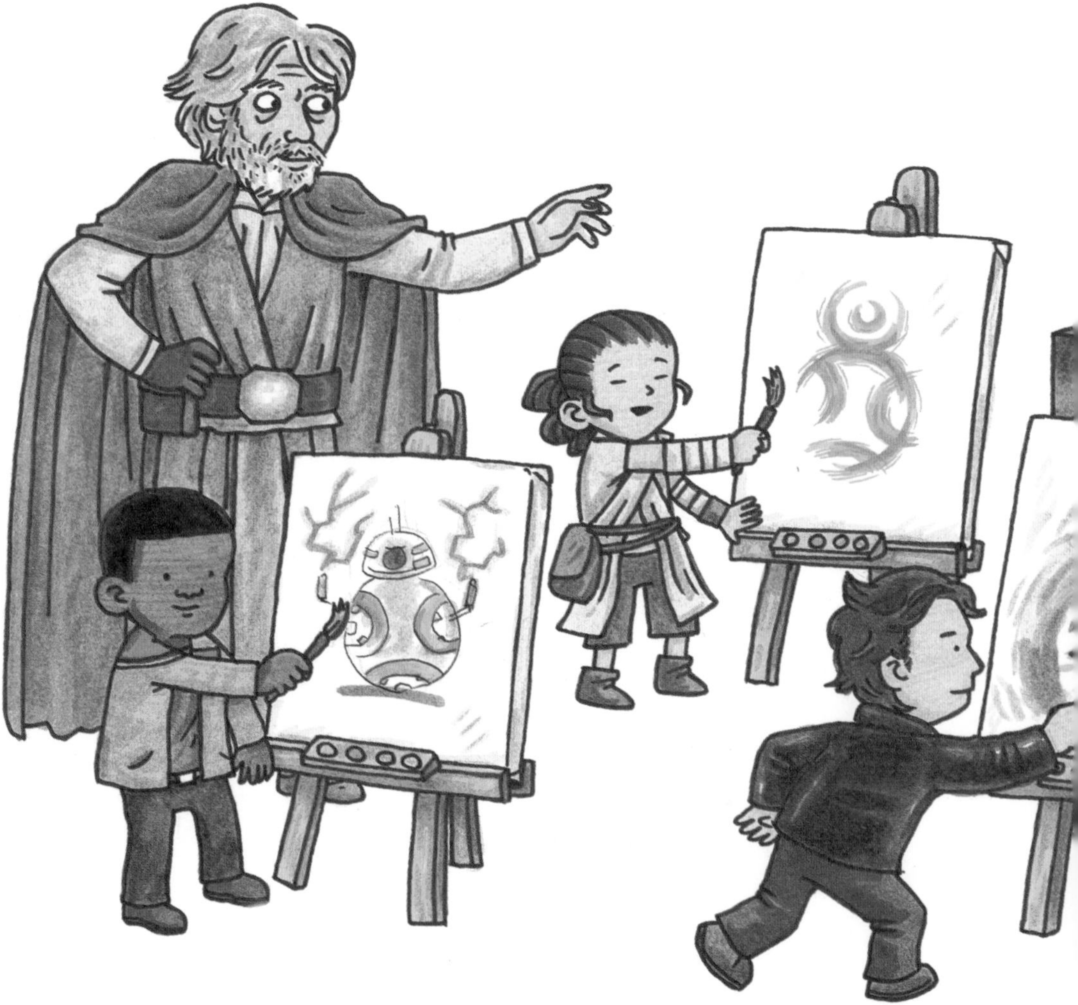

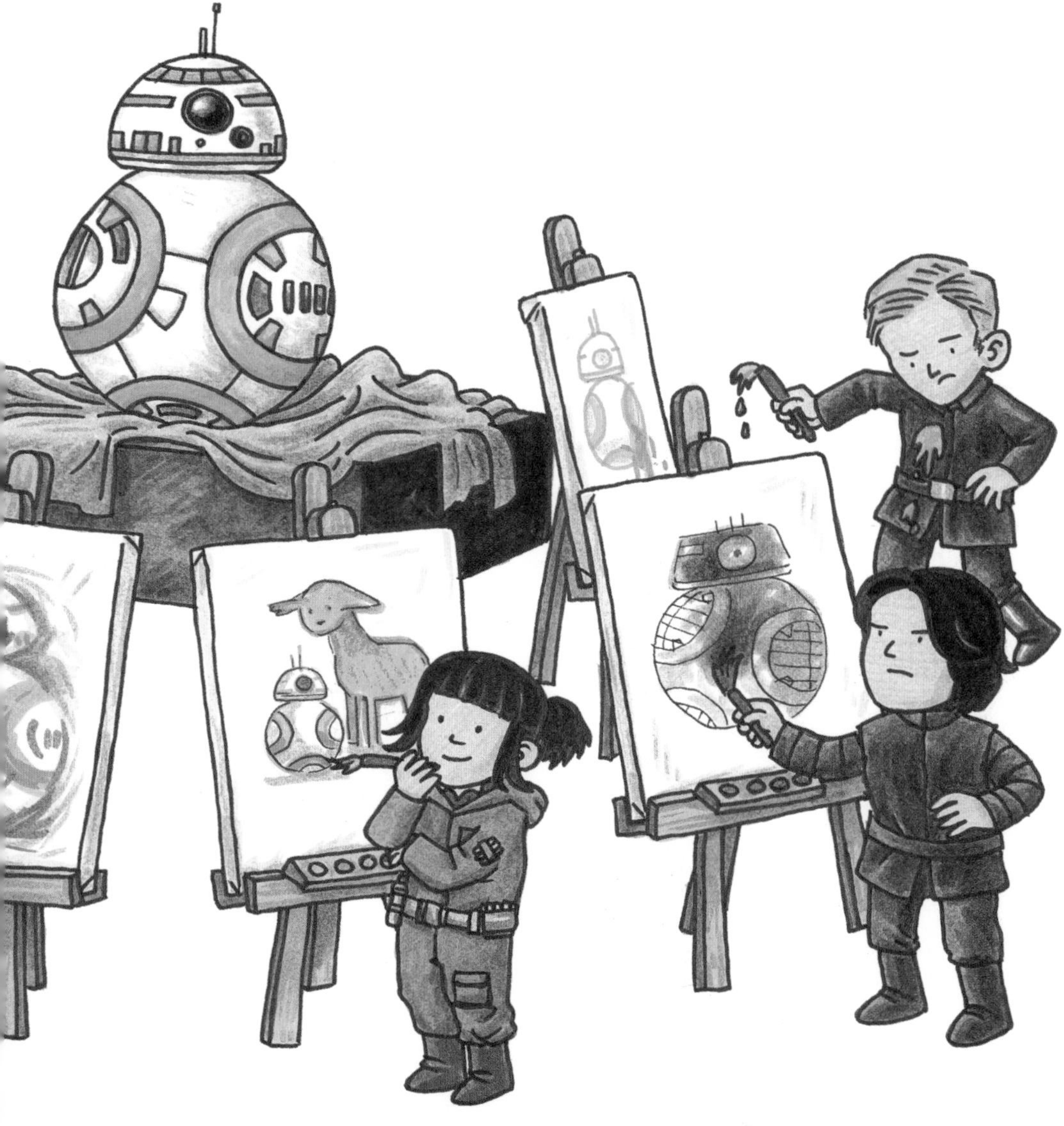

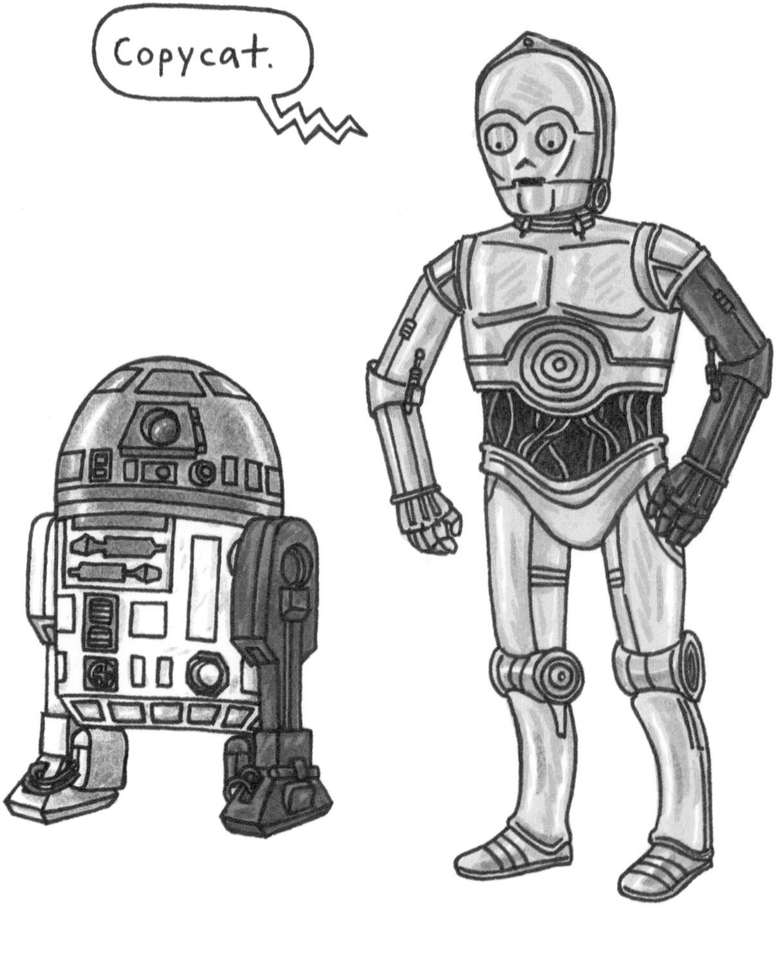
Copycat.

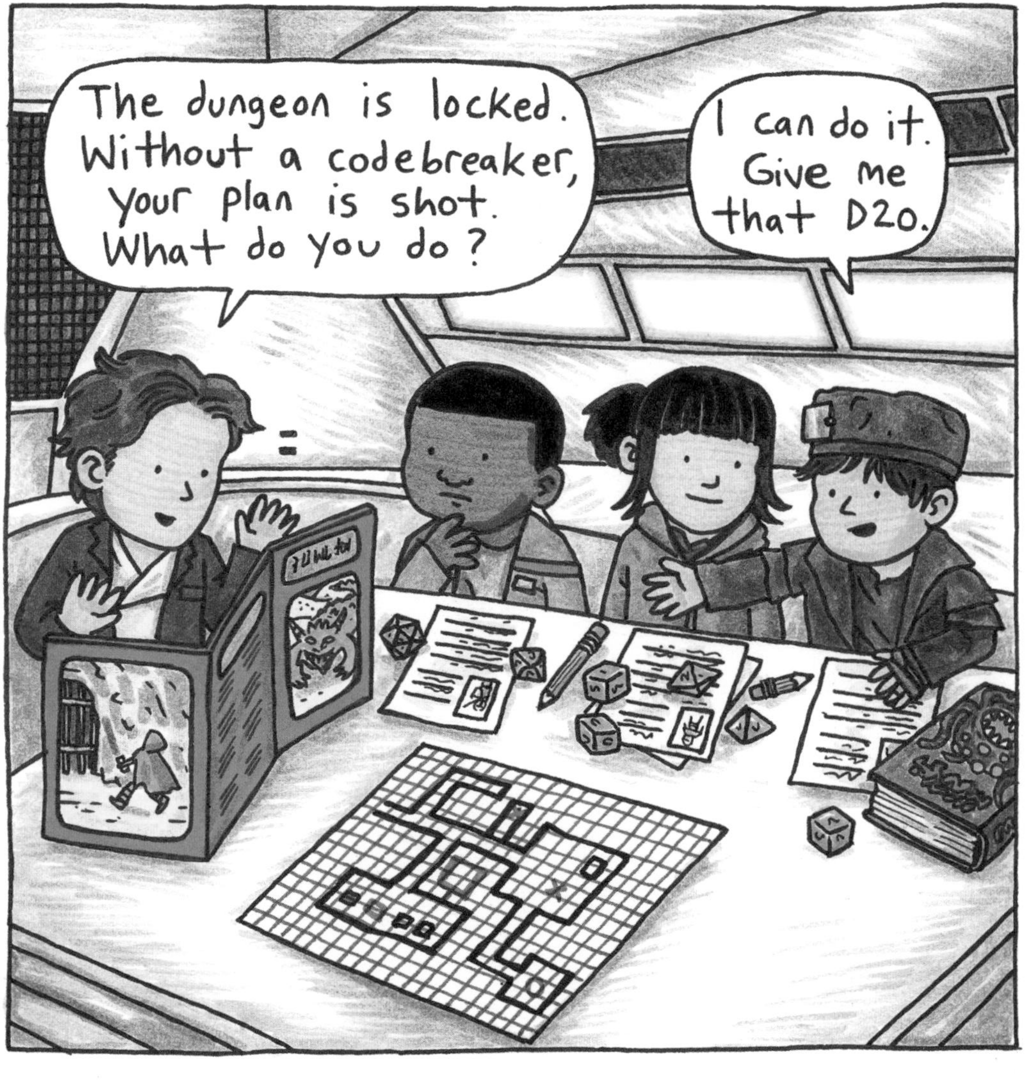
The dungeon is locked. Without a codebreaker, your plan is shot. What do you do?
I can do it. Give me that D20.

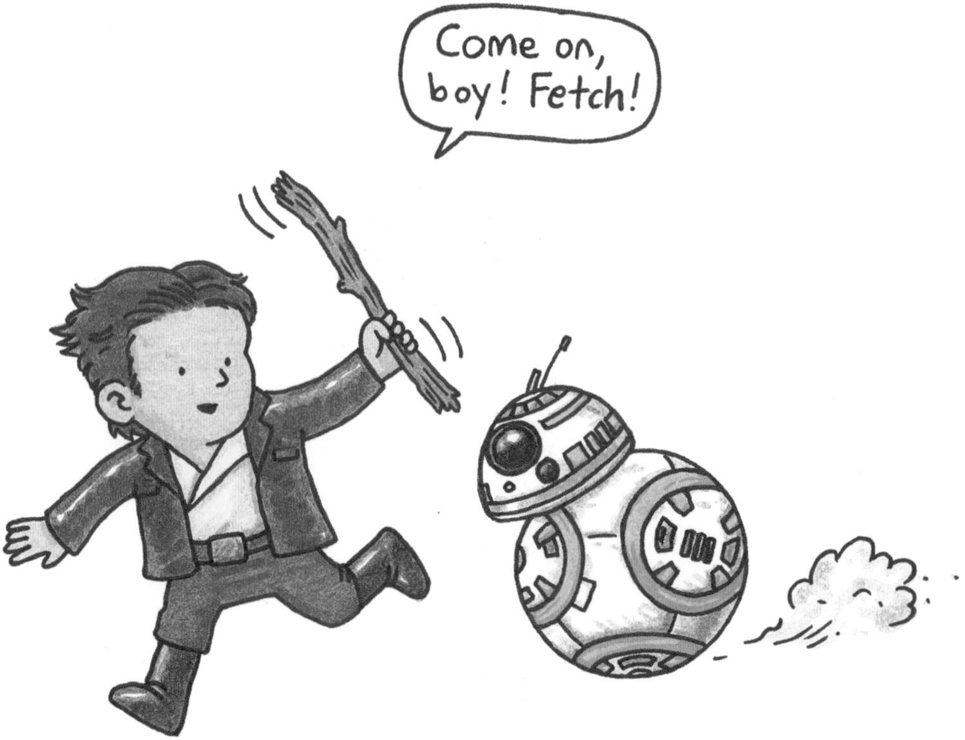
Come on, boy! Fetch!

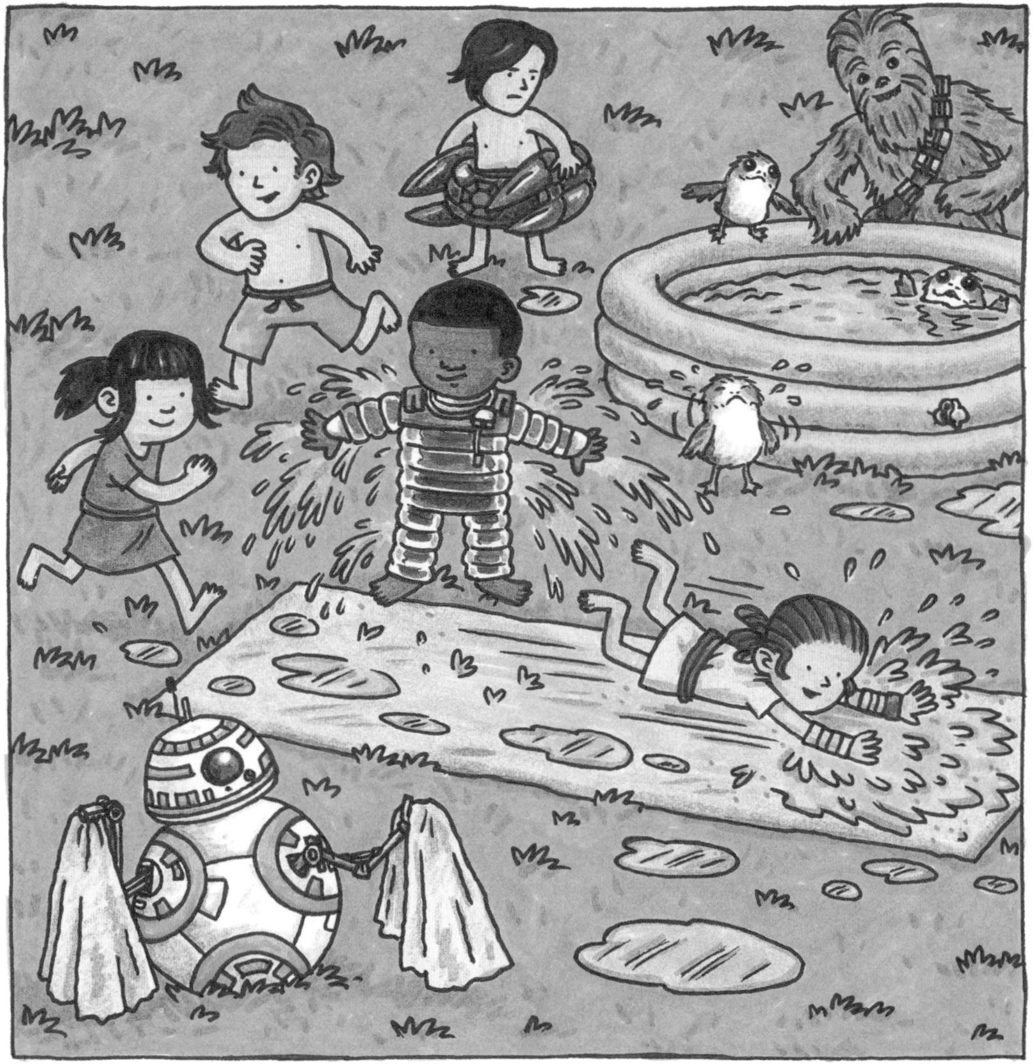

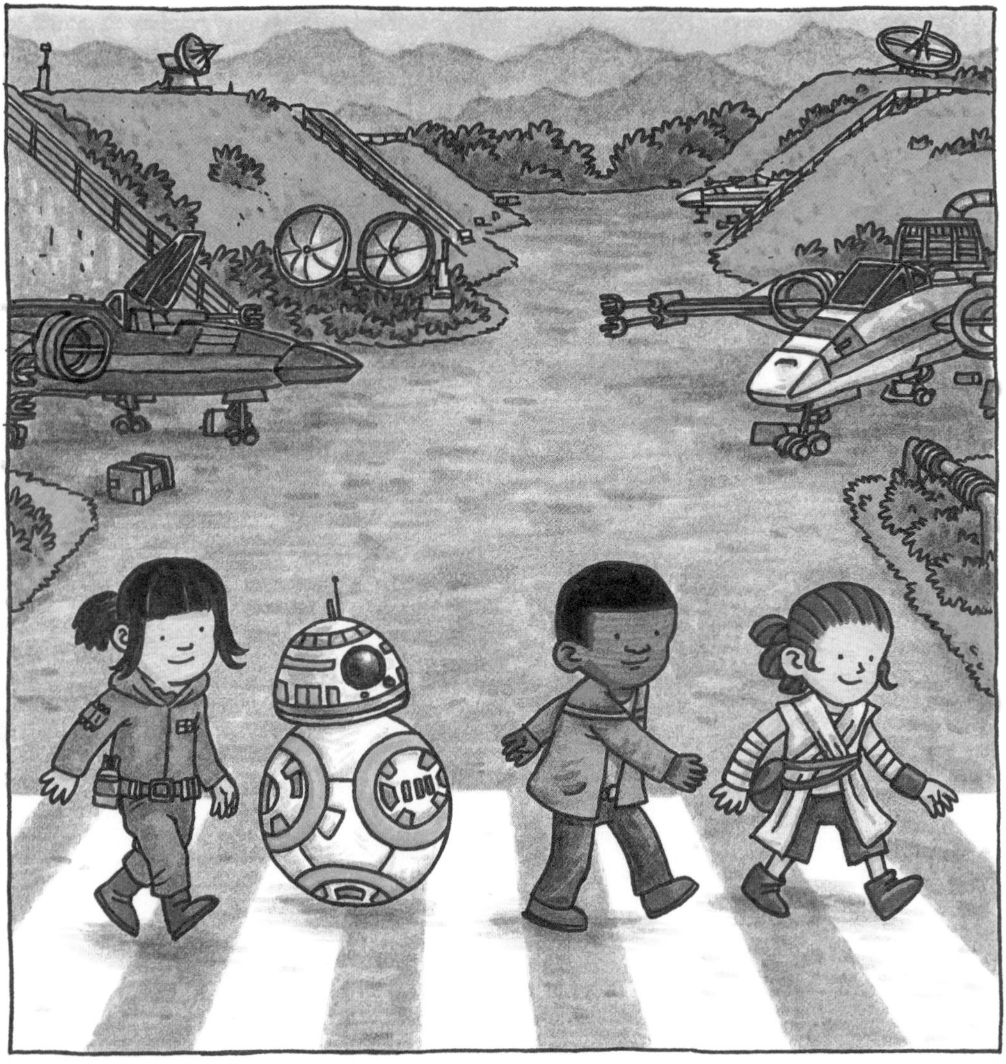

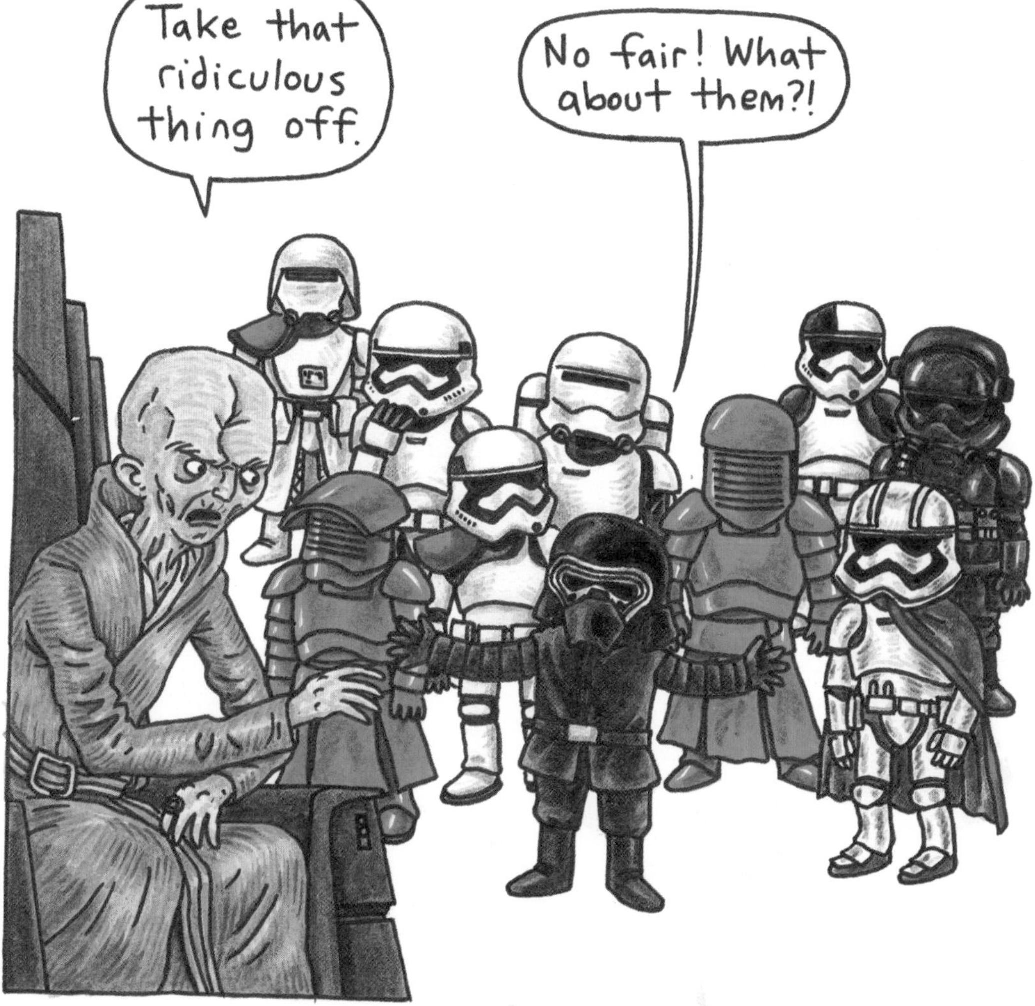
Take that ridiculous thing off.
No fair! What about them?!

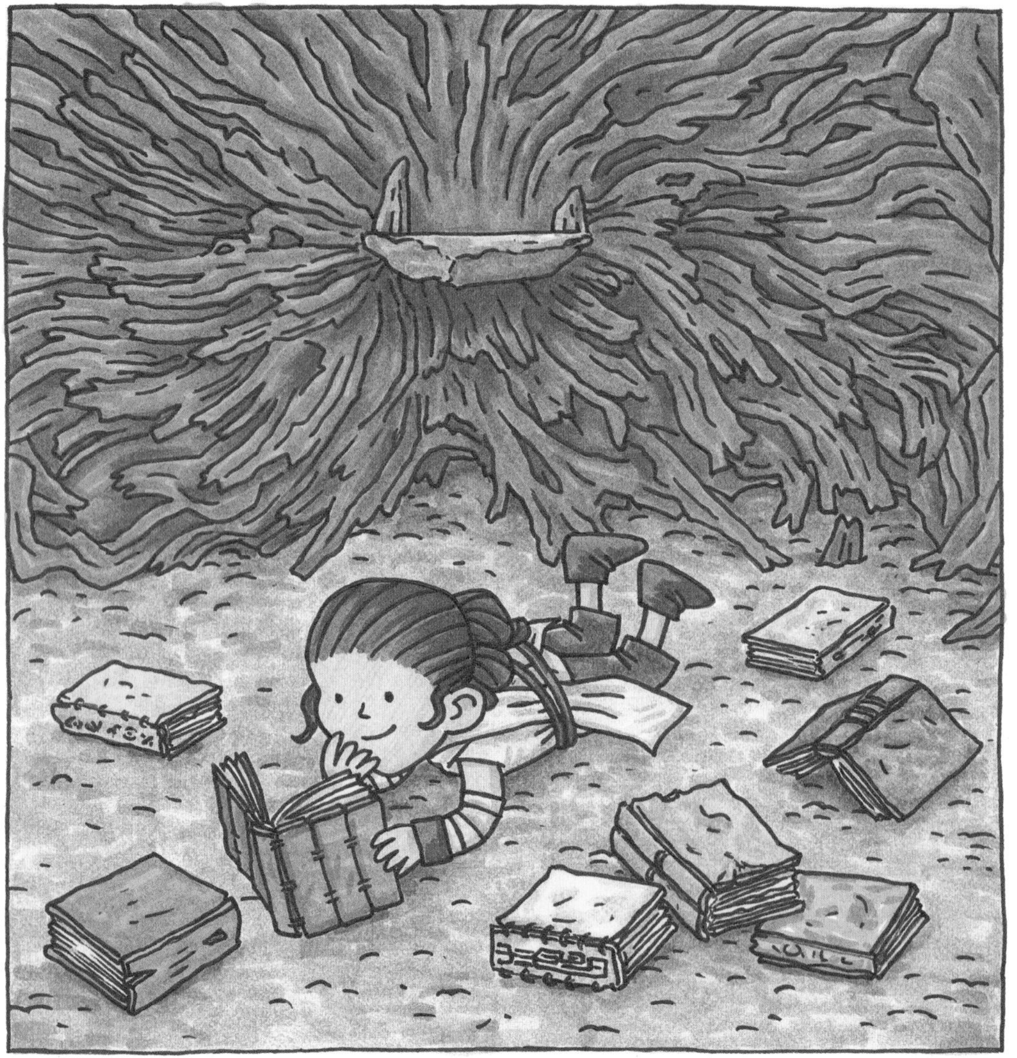

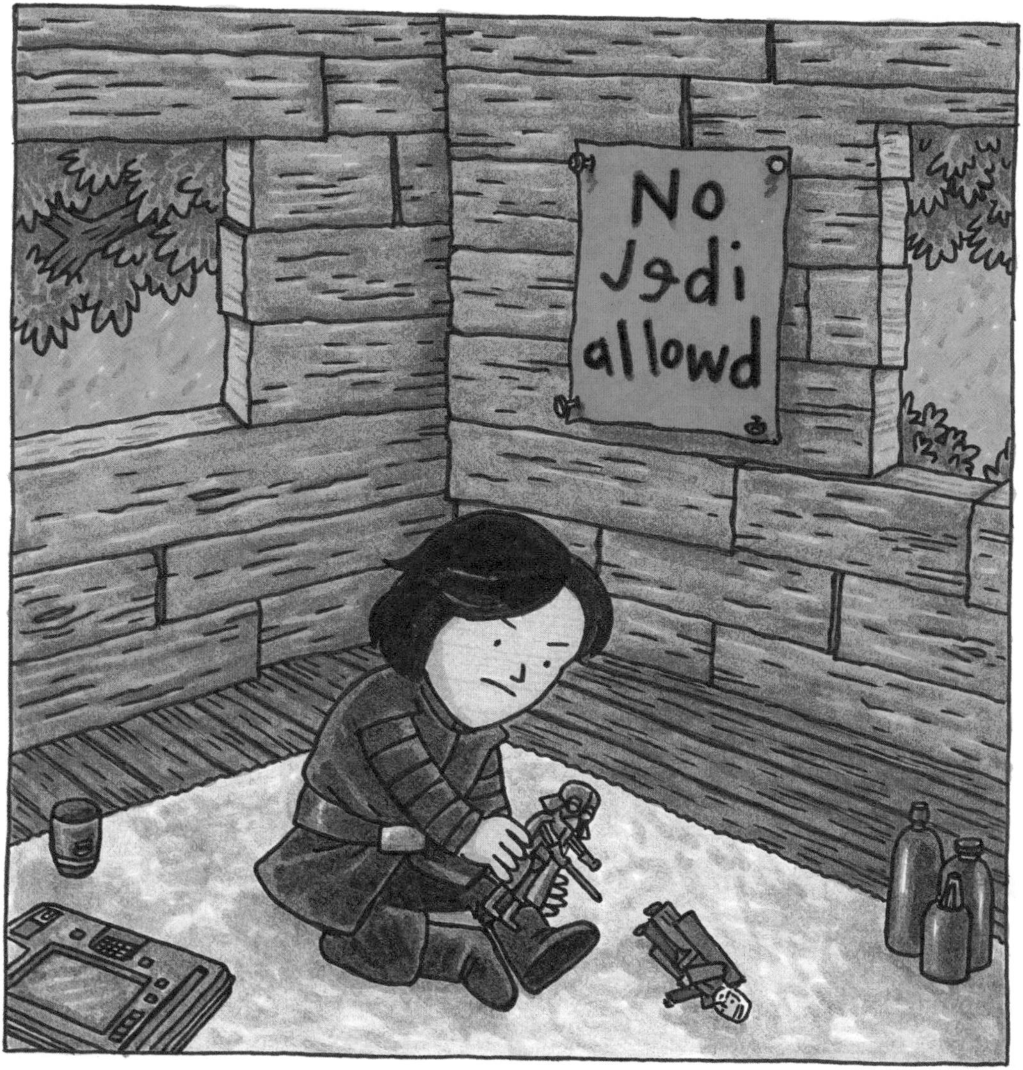
No
Jedi
allowd

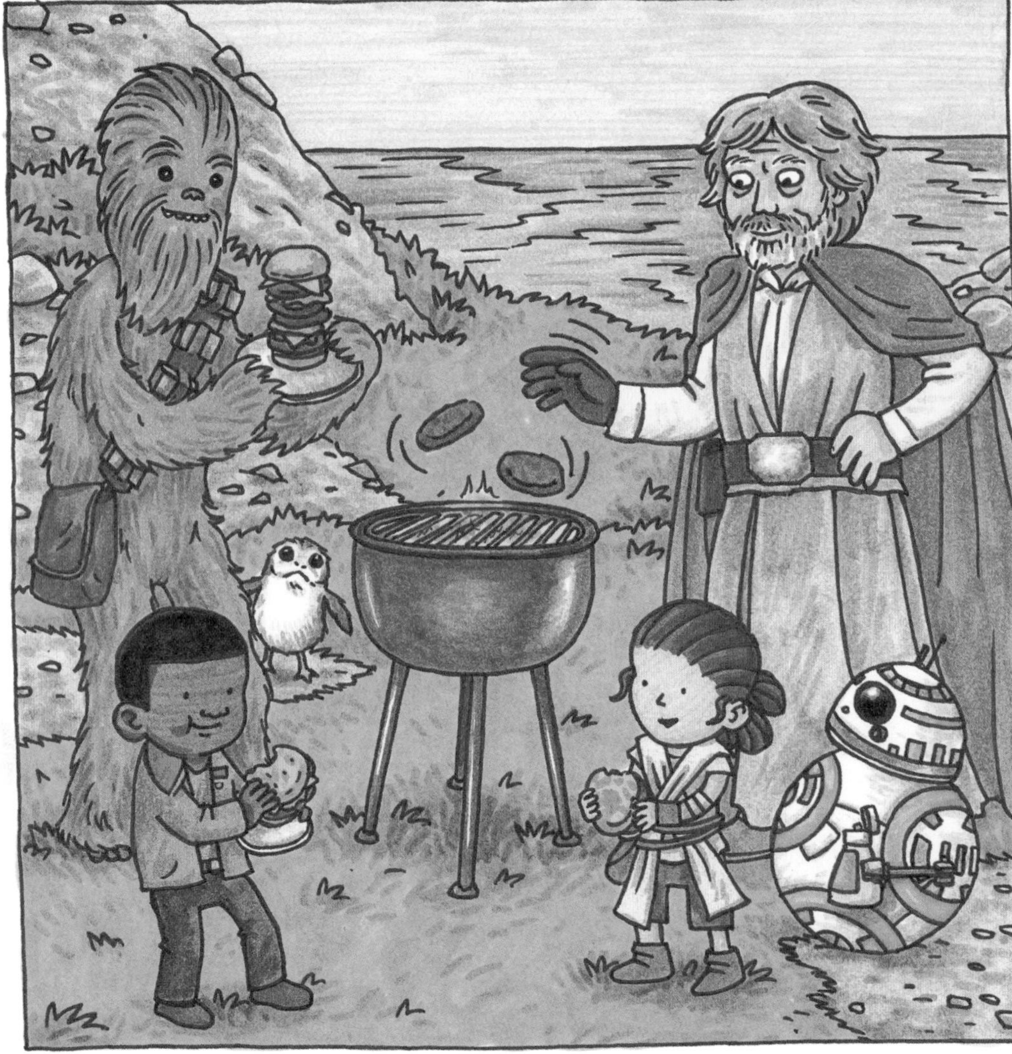

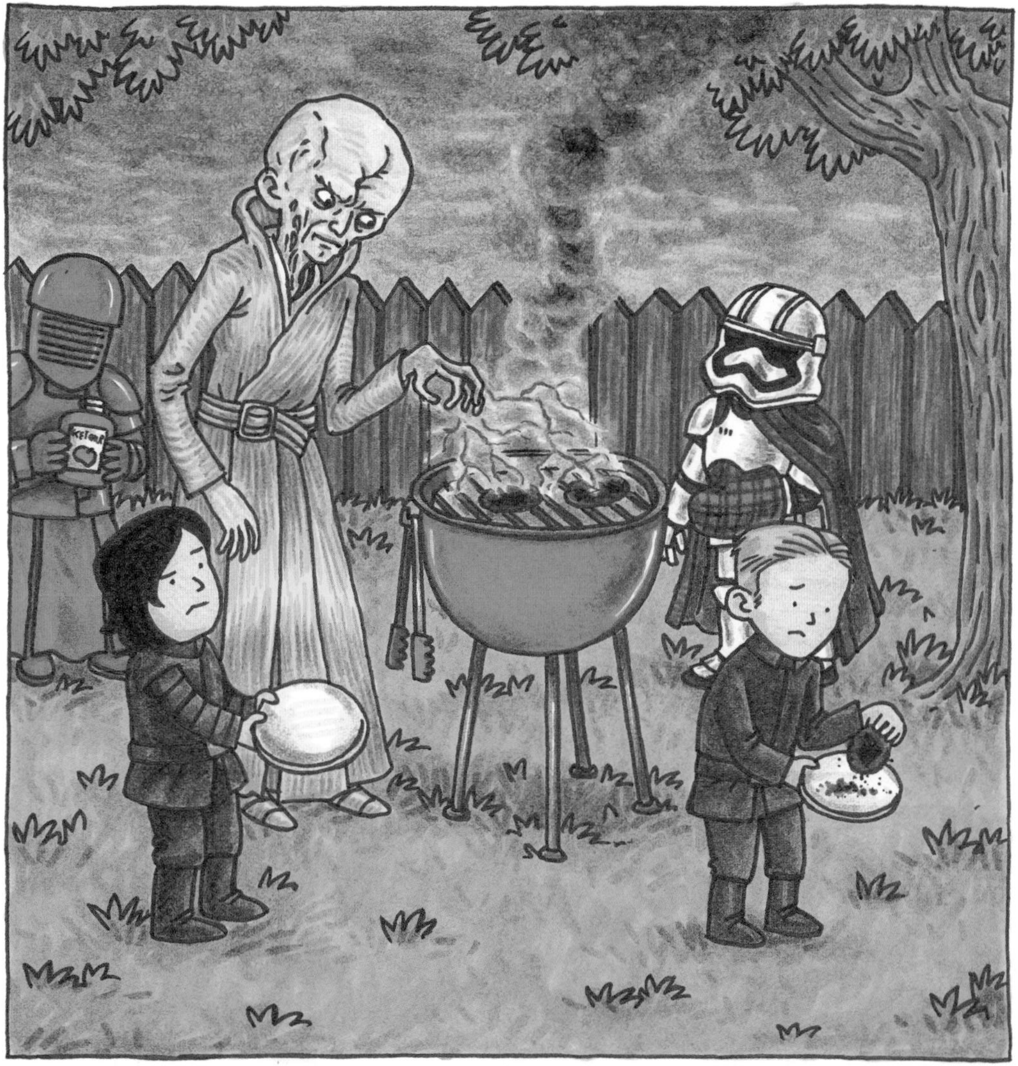

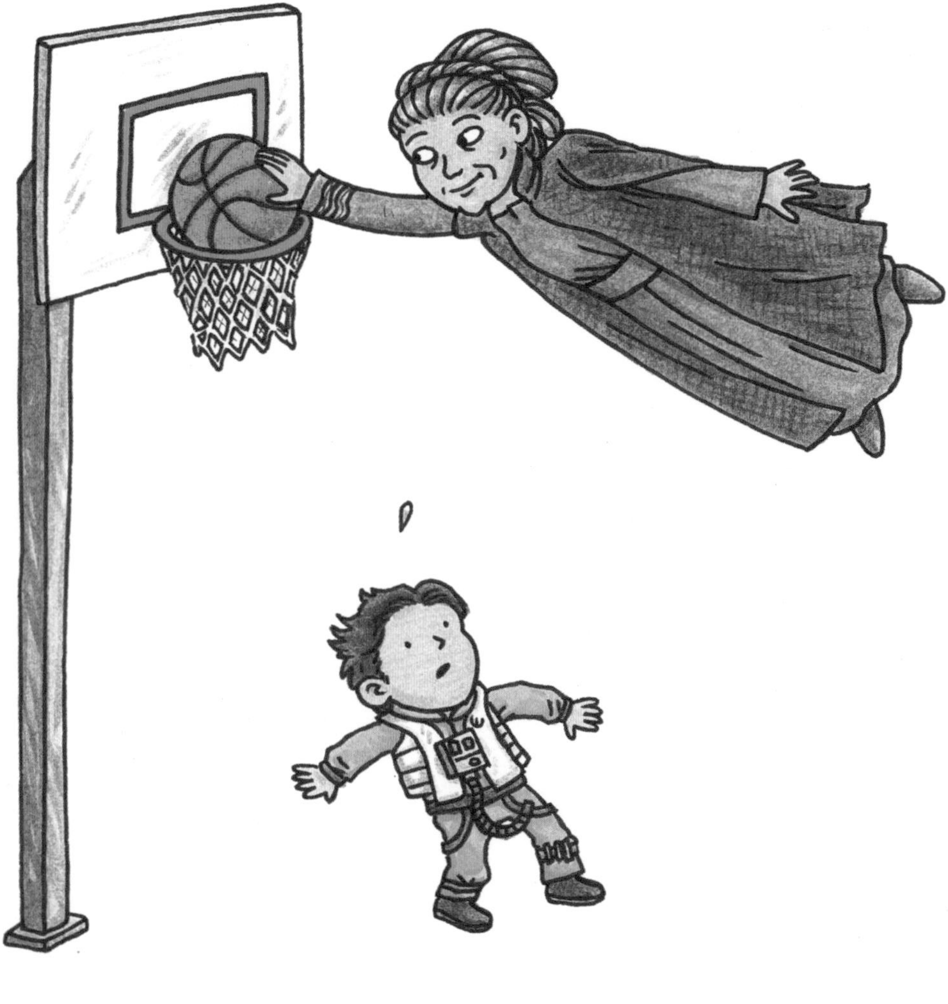

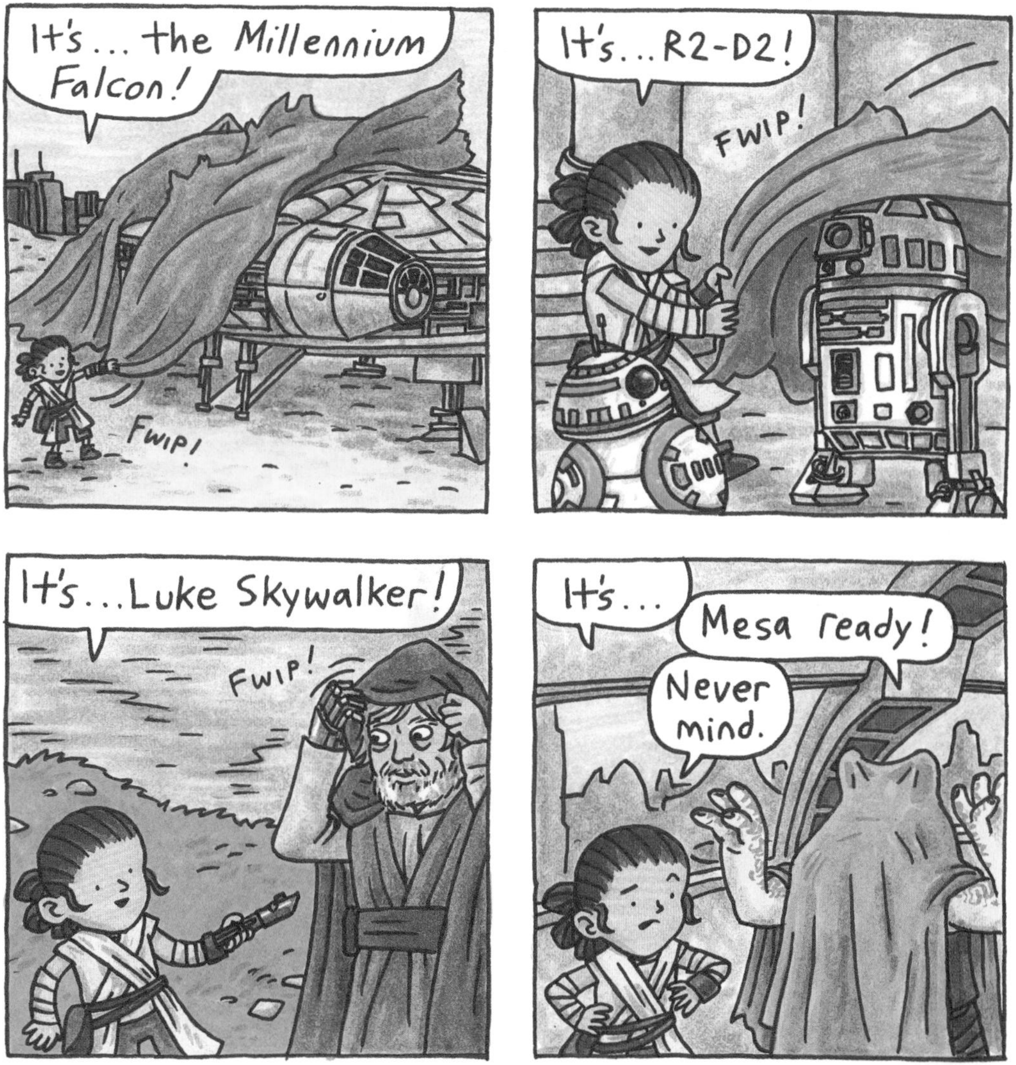
It's... the Millennium Falcon!
FWIP!
It's... R2-D2!
FWIP!
It's...Luke Skywalker!
FWIP!
It's...
Mesa ready!
Never mind.

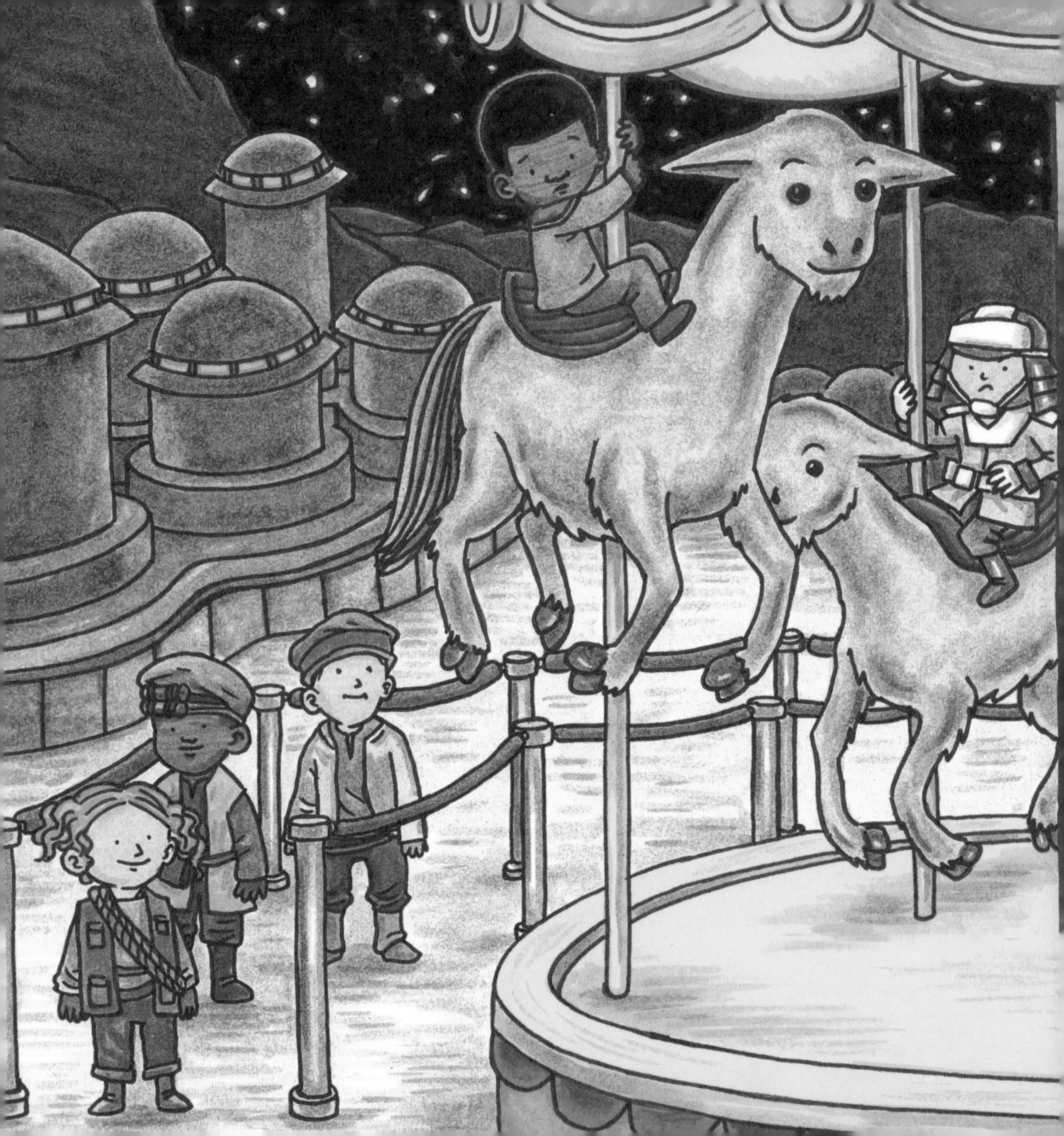

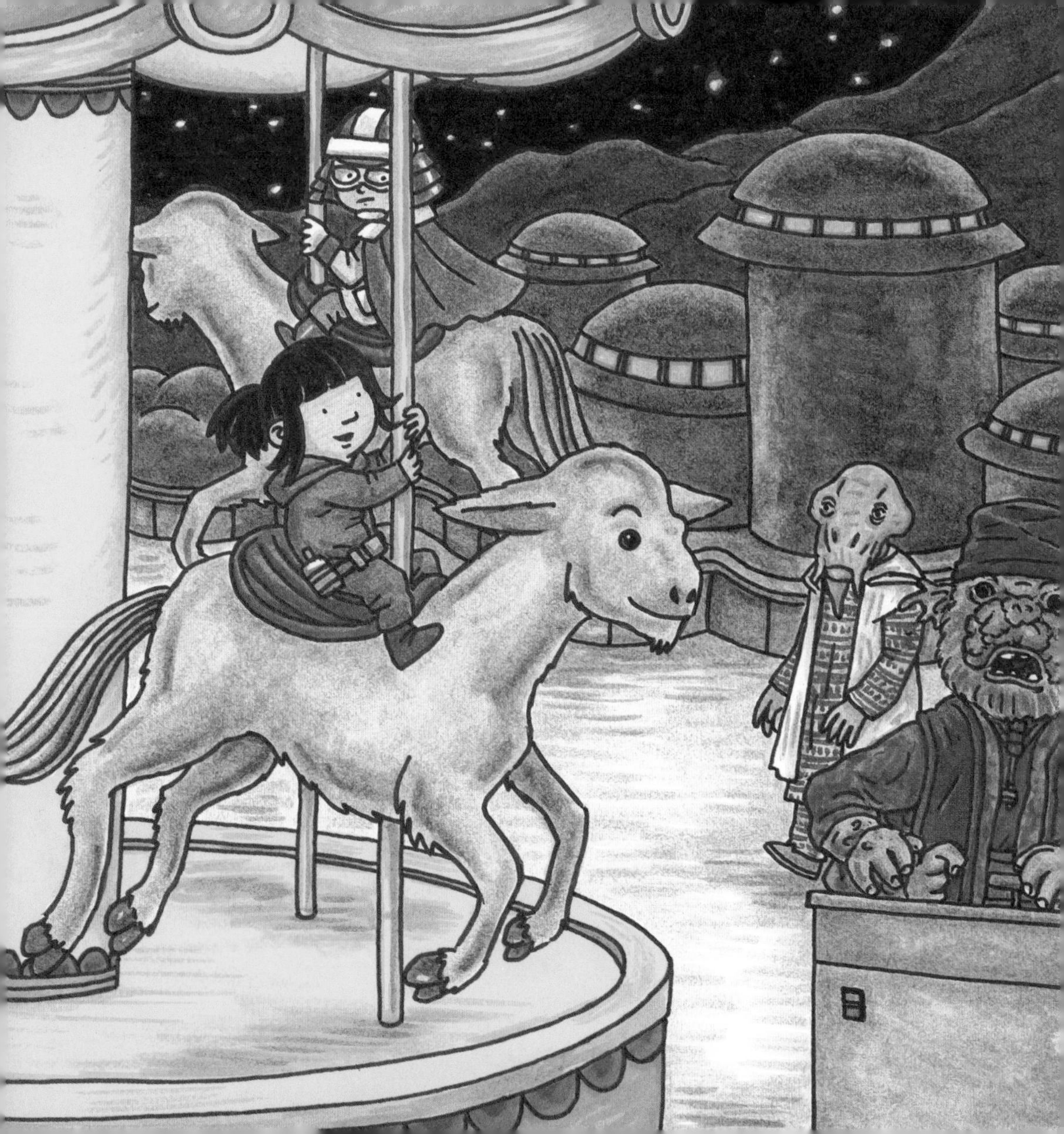

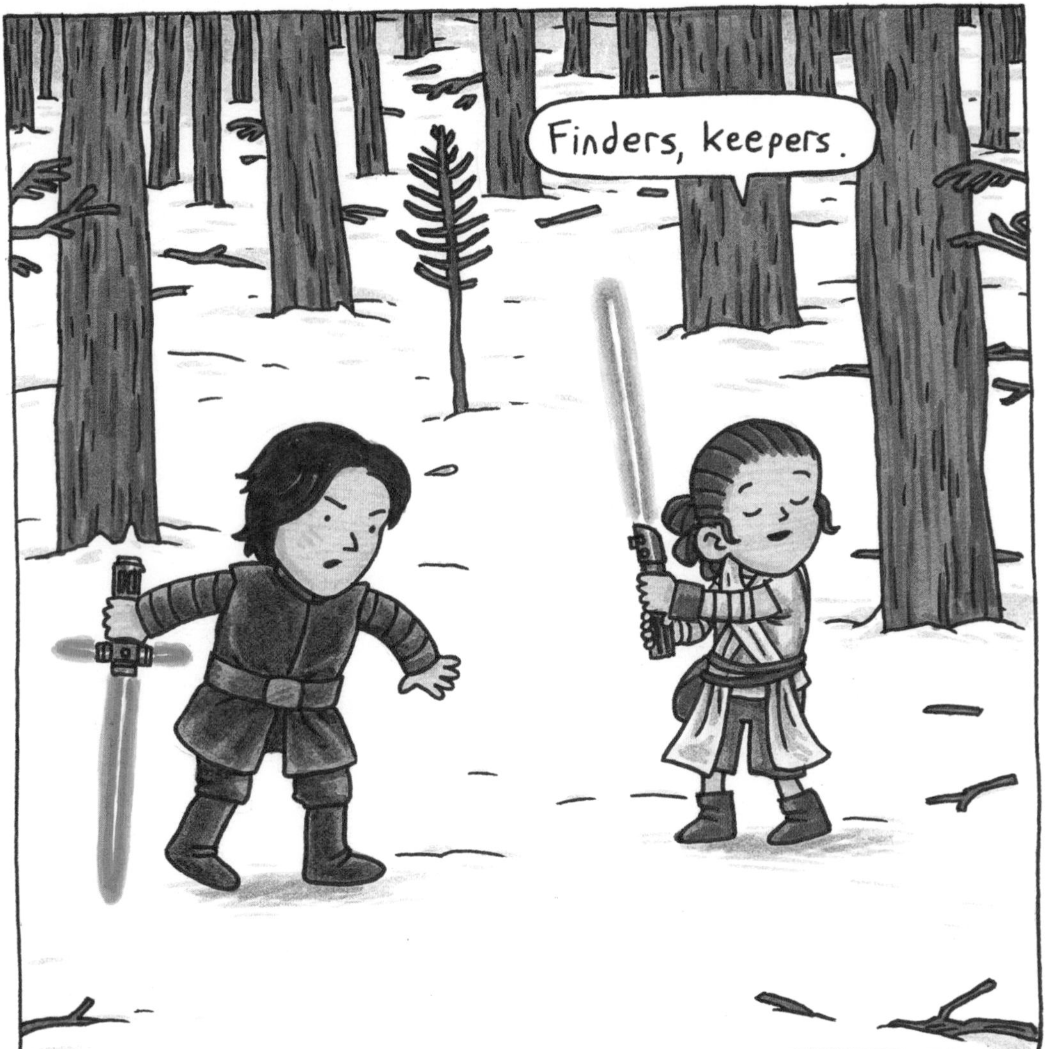
Finders, keepers.

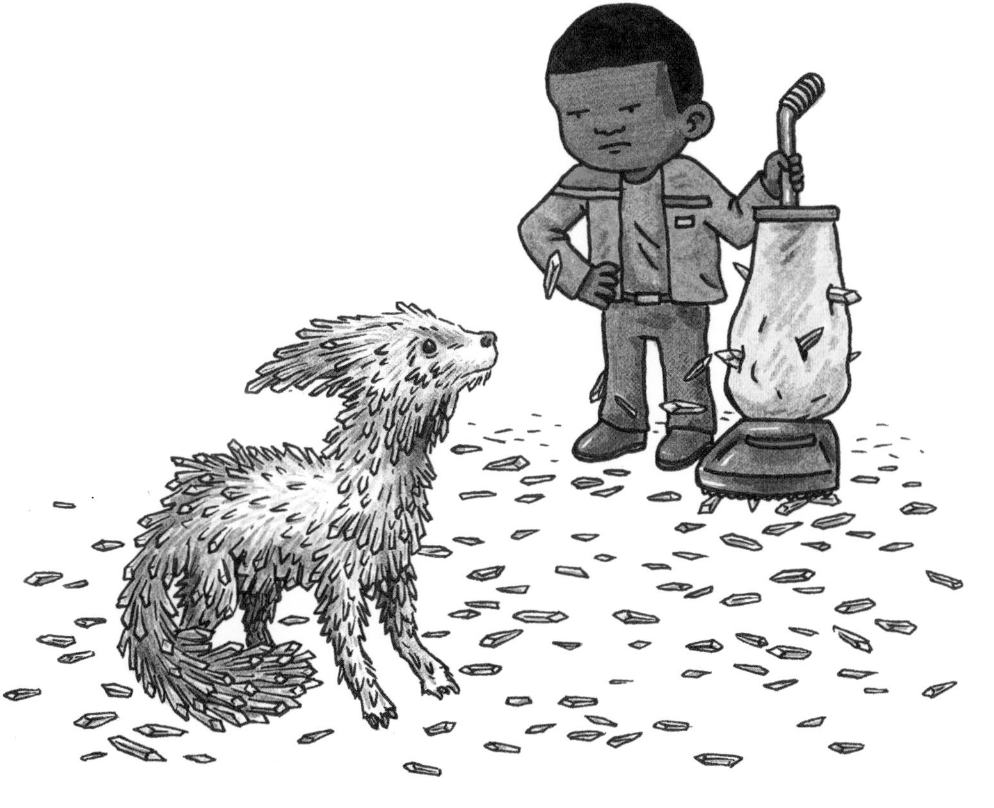

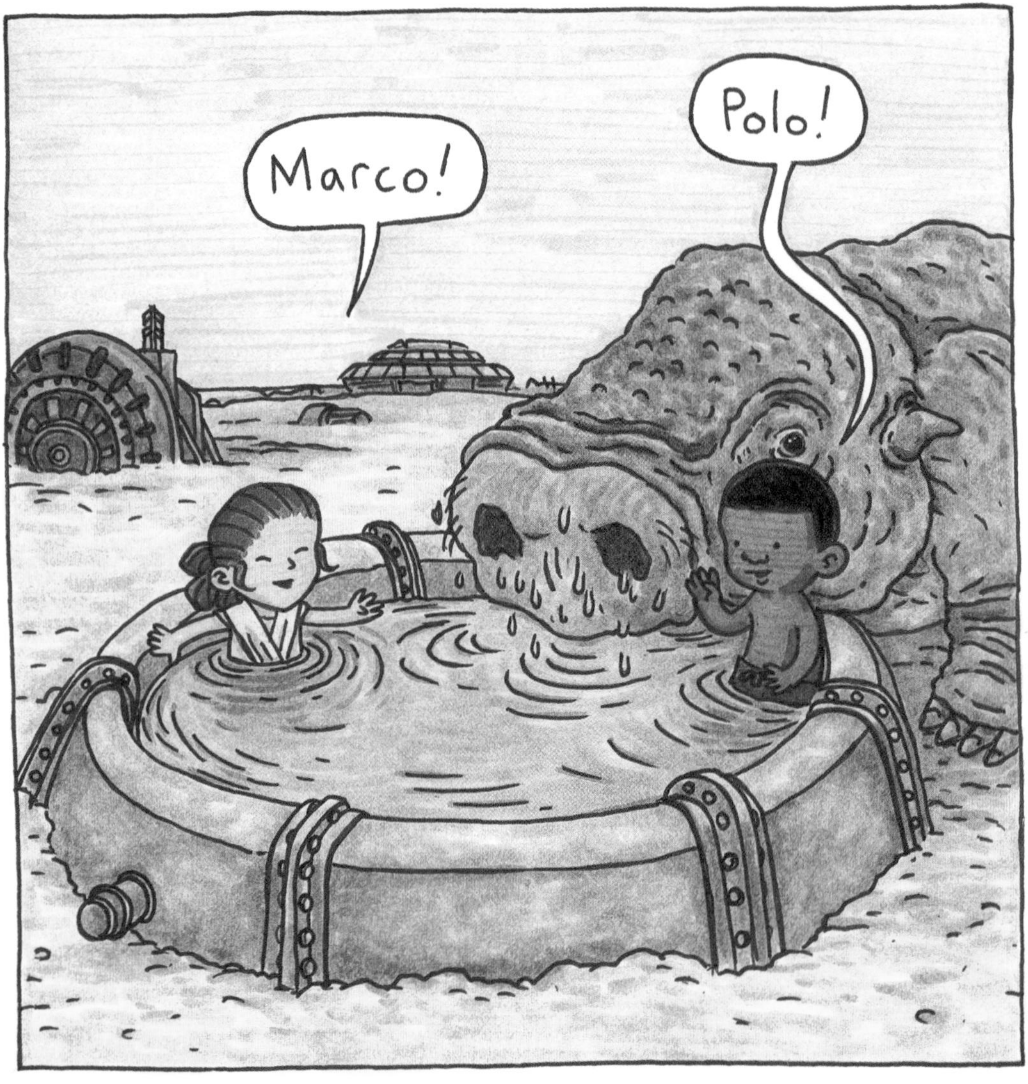
Marco!
Polo!

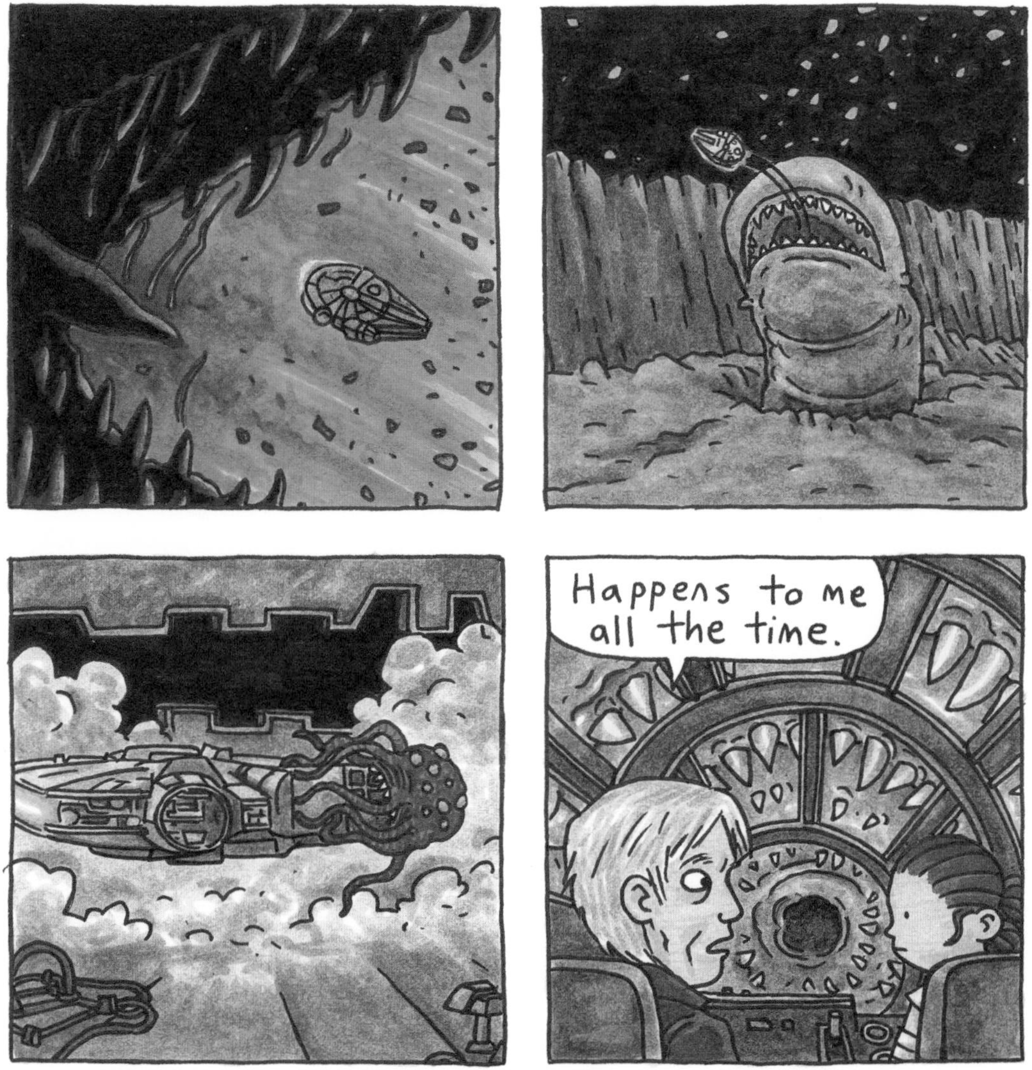
Happens to me all the time.

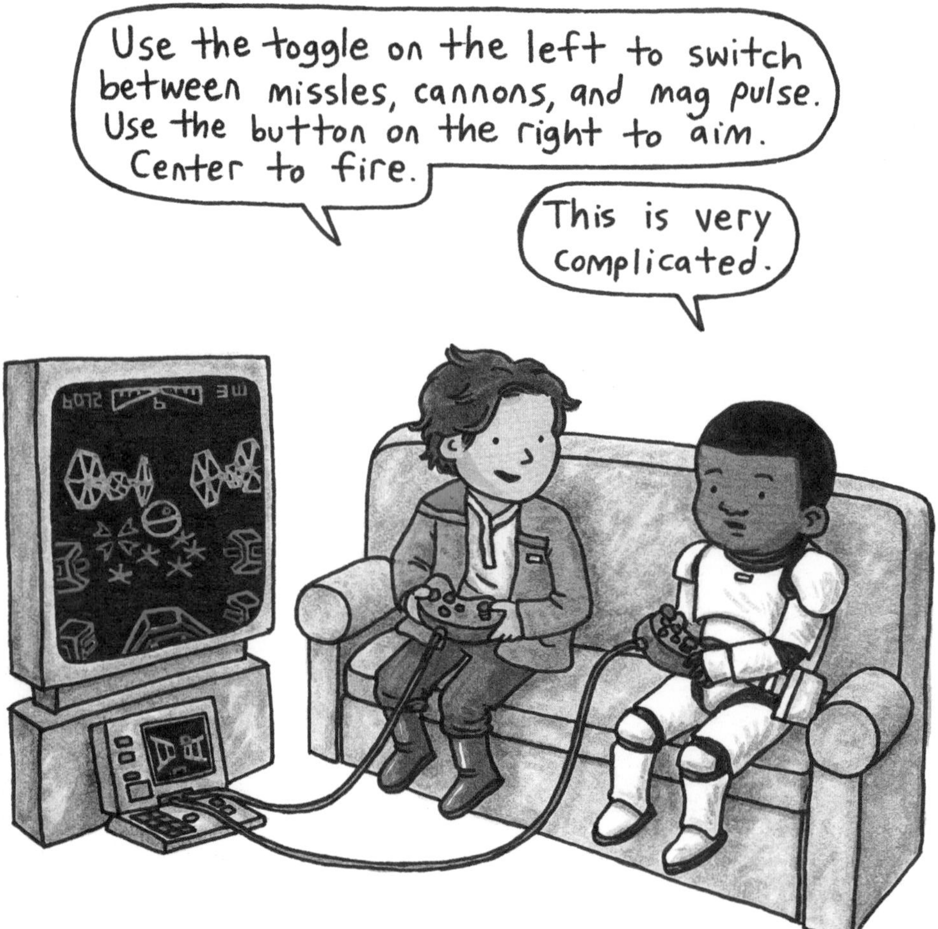
Use the toggle on the left to switch between missles, cannons, and mag pulse. Use the button on the right to aim. Center to fire.
This is very complicated.

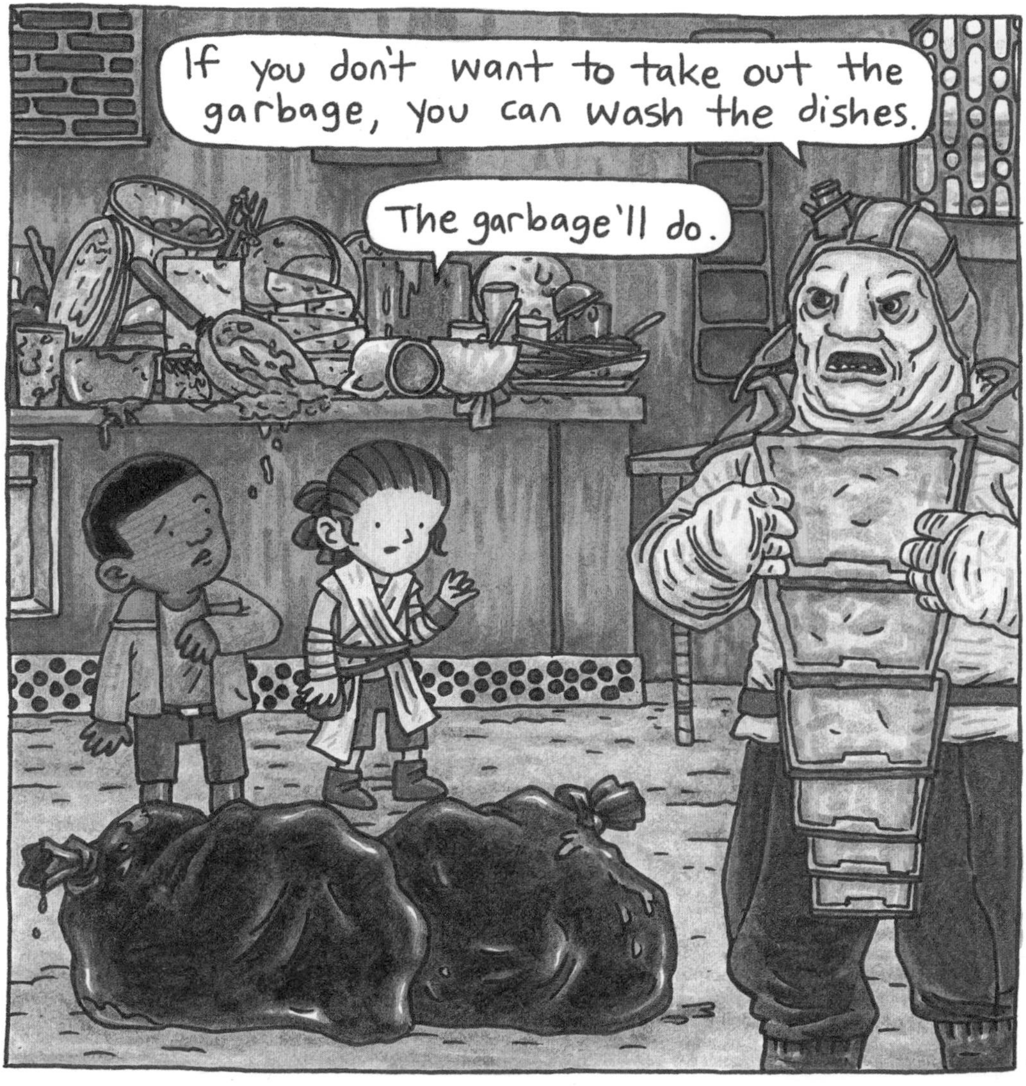
If you don't want to take out the garbage, you can wash the dishes.
The garbage'll do.

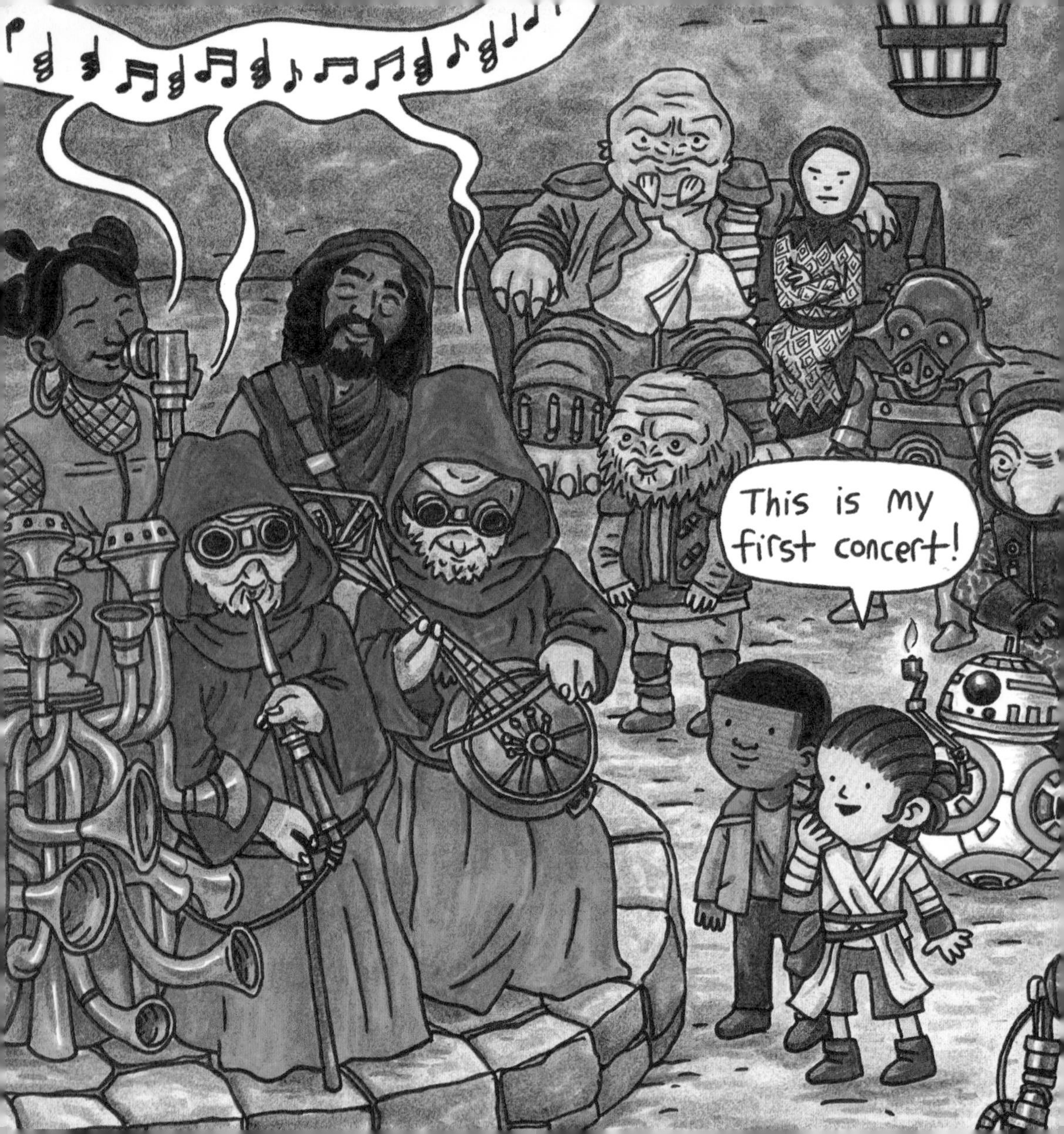
This is my first concert!

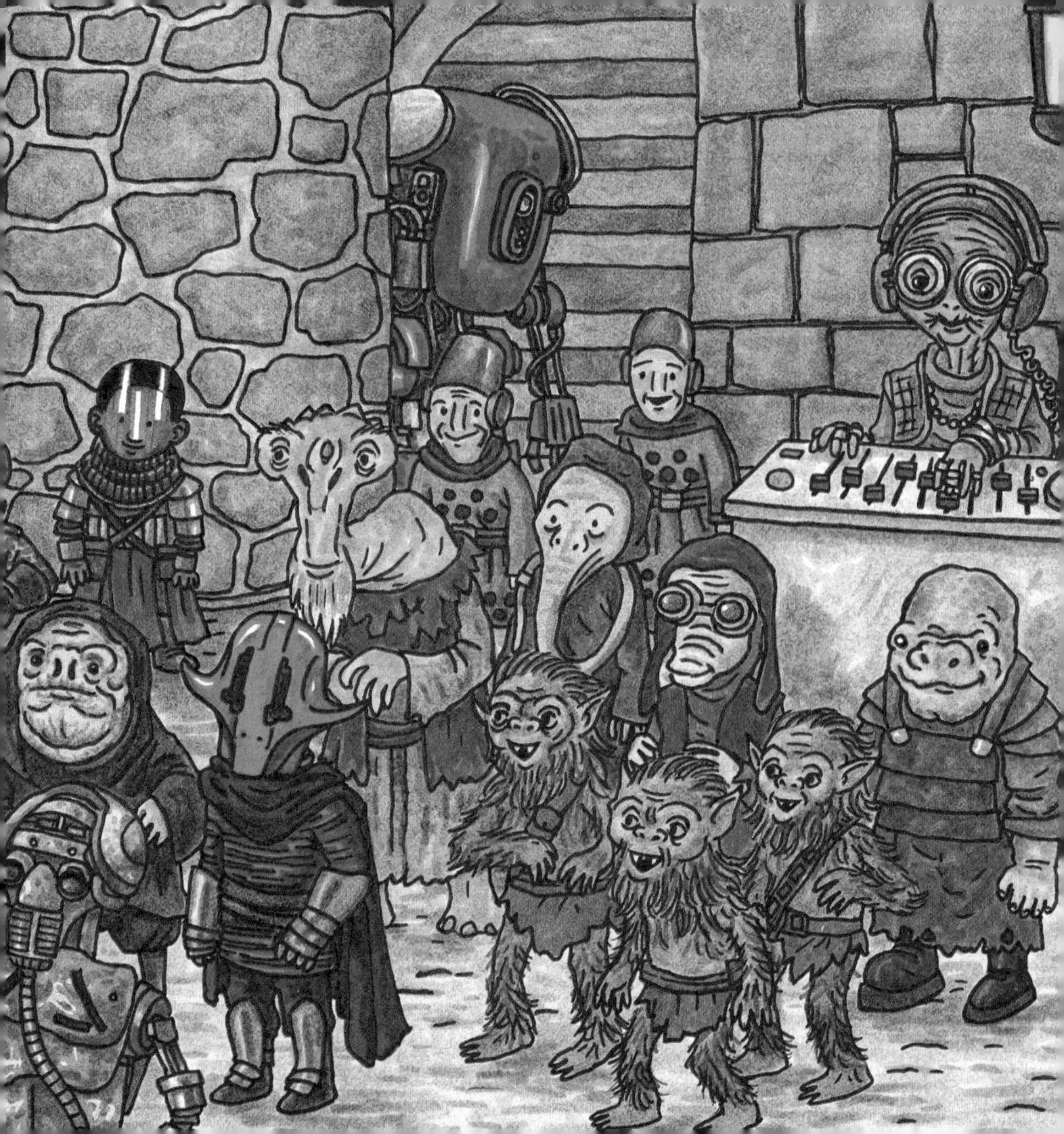

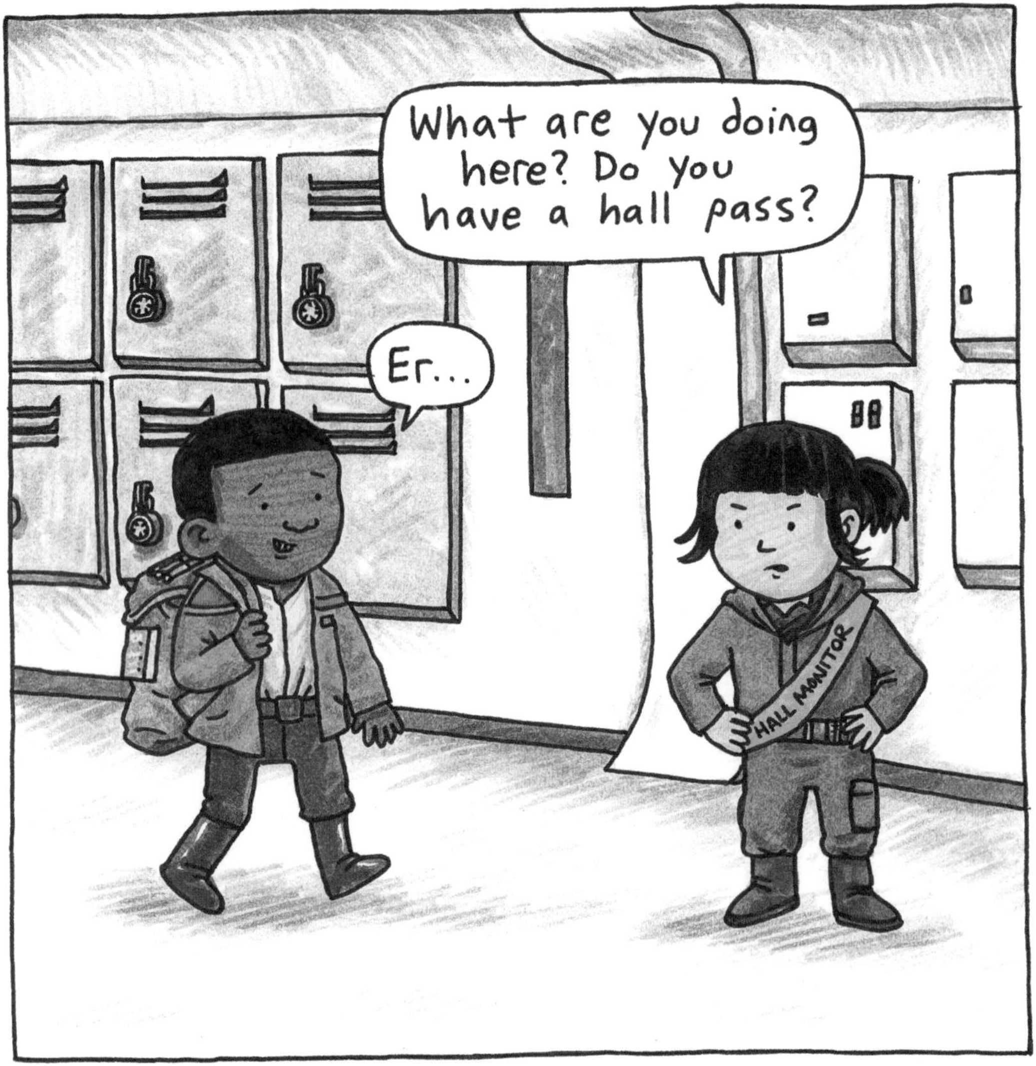
What are you doing here? Do you have a hall pass?
Er...
HALL MONITOR

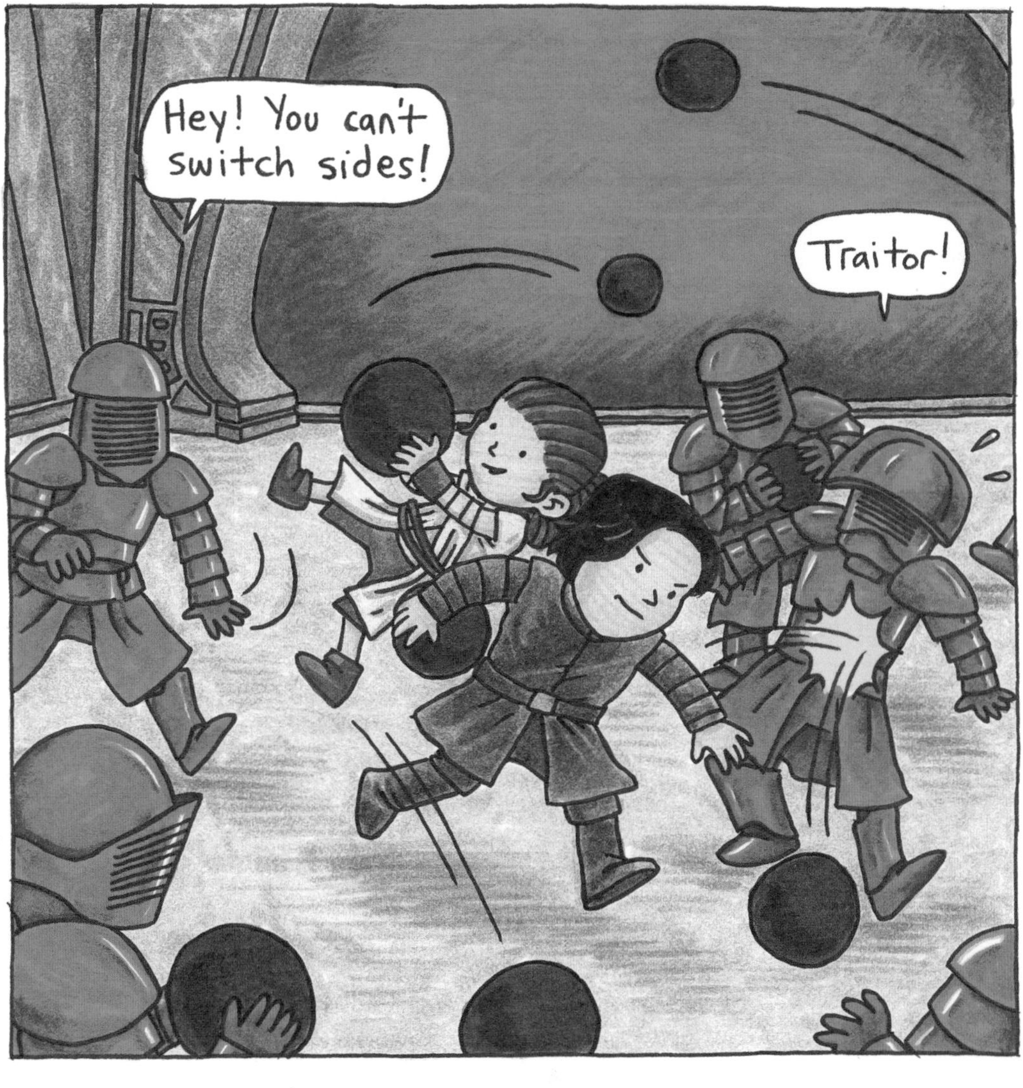
Hey! You can't switch sides!
Traitor!

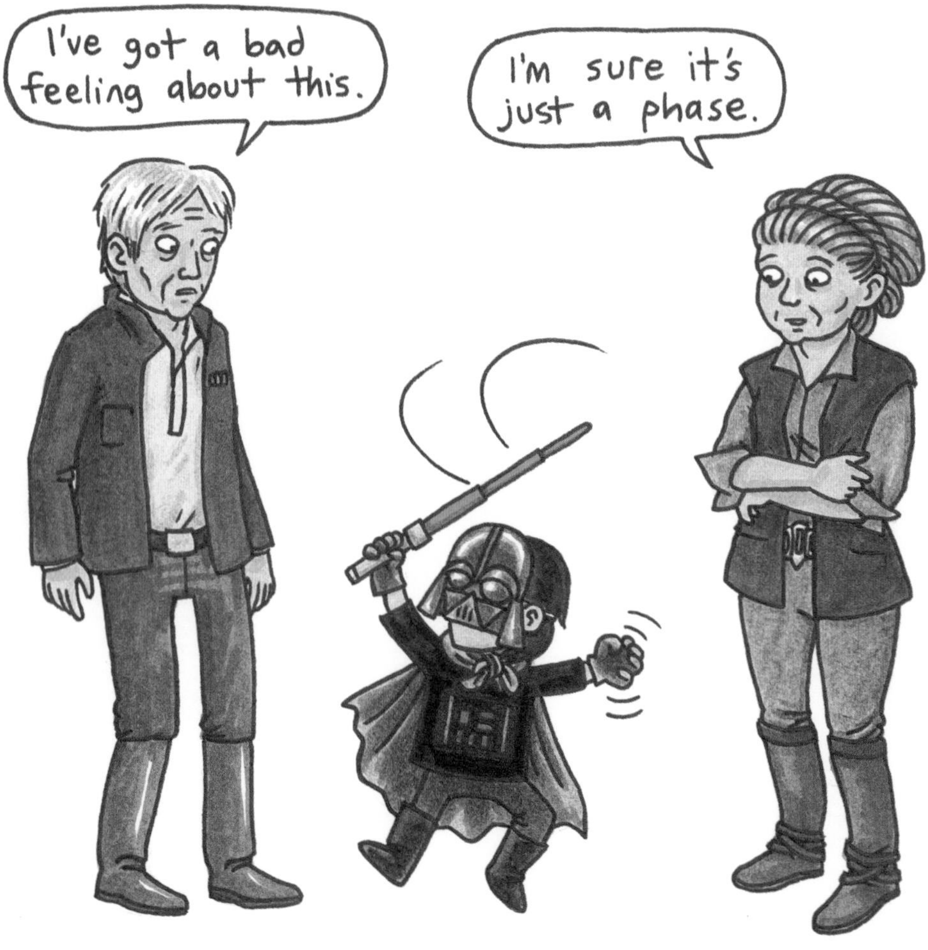
I've got a bad feeling about this.
I'm sure it's just a phase.

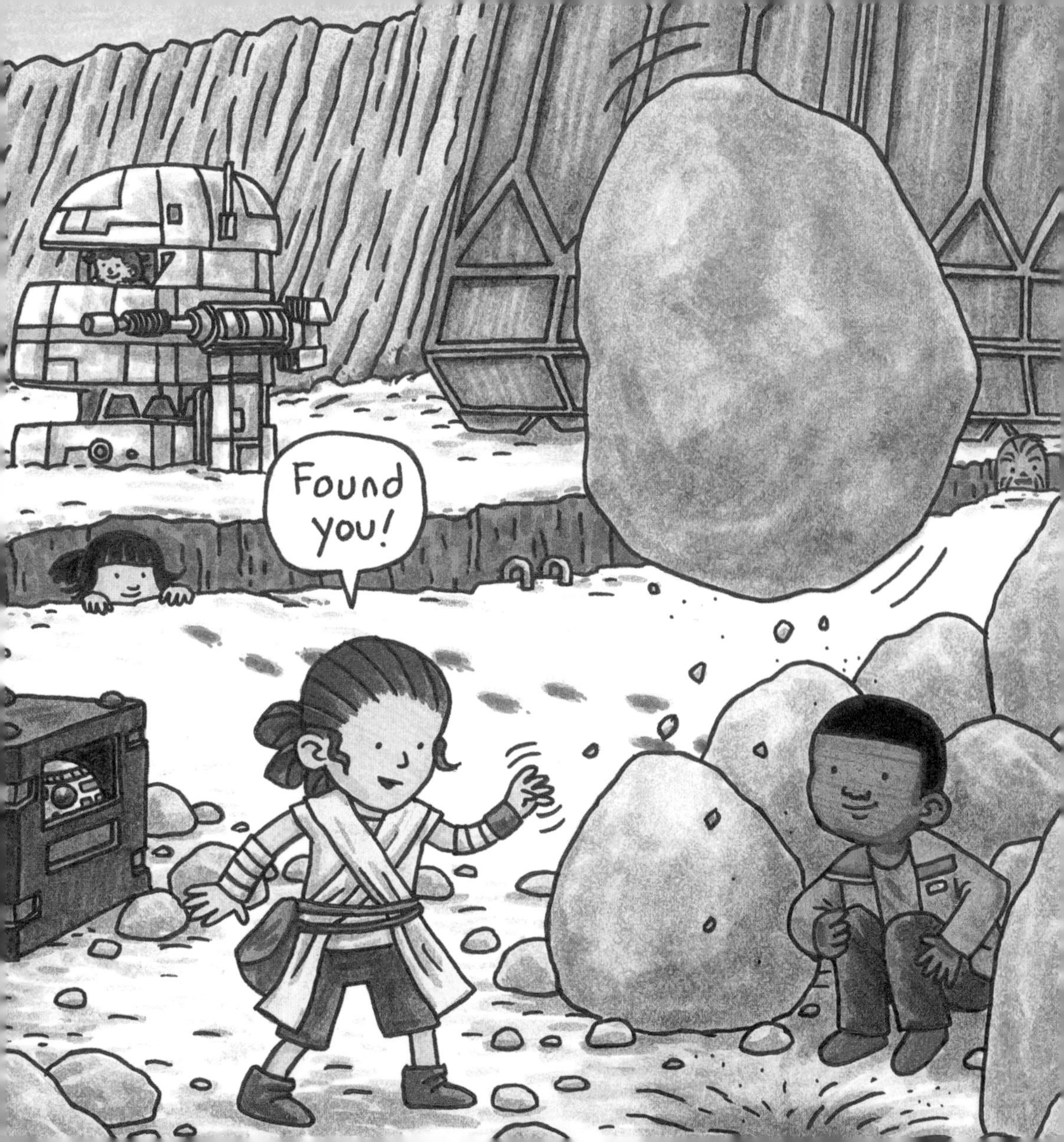
Found you!

Jeffrey Brown is the author of numerous middle grade graphic novels and autobiographical comics. He lives in Chicago with his wife and two sons.

P.O. BOX 120
DEERFIELD IL
60015-0120
USA

www.jeffreybrowncomics.com

ALSO BY JEFFREY BROWN
FROM CHRONICLE BOOKS:

Darth Vader and Friends
Goodnight Darth Vader
Kids Are Weird
Vader's Little Princess
Darth Vader and Son
Cats Are Weird
Cat Getting Out of a Bag
www.chroniclebooks.com

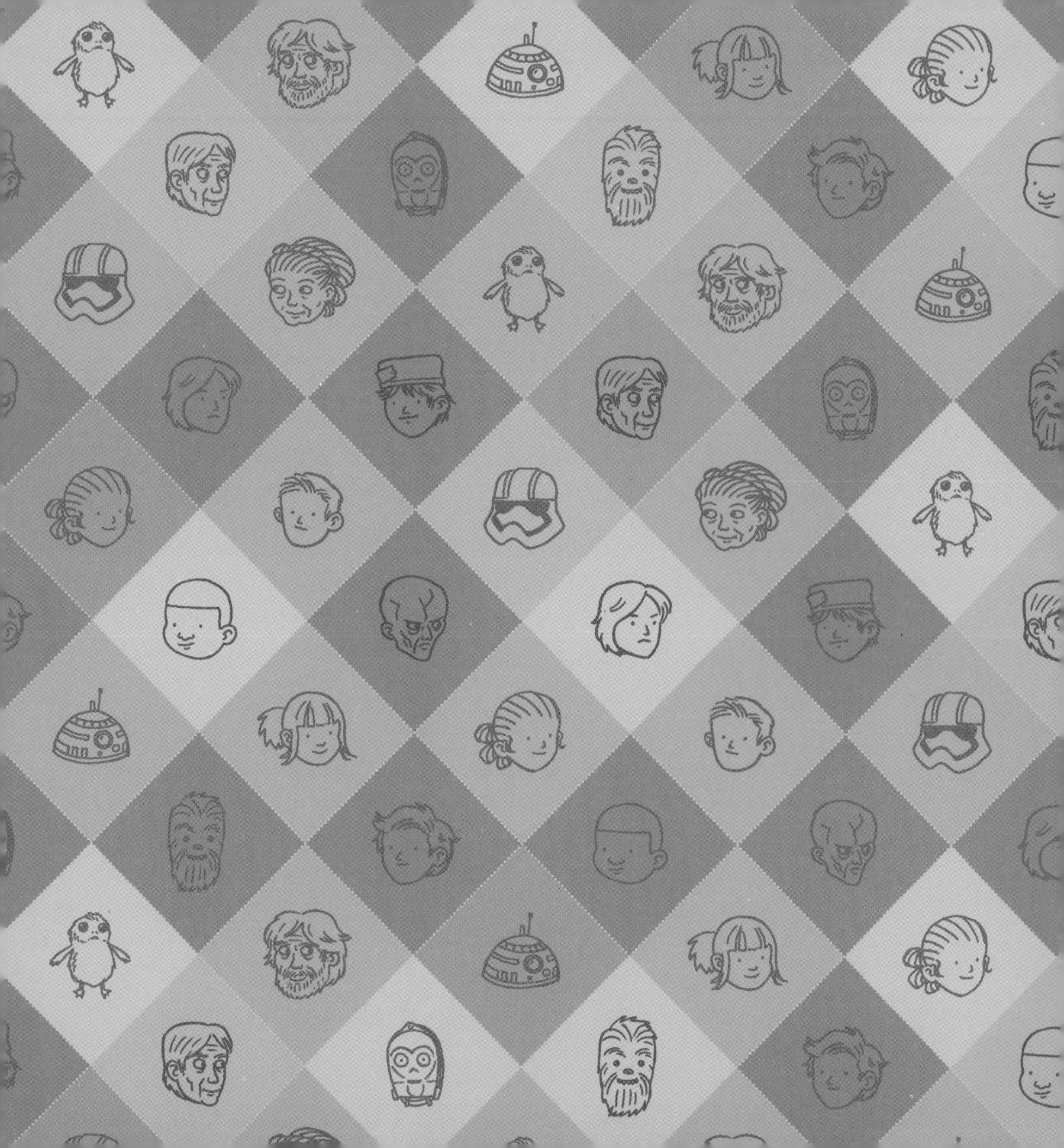

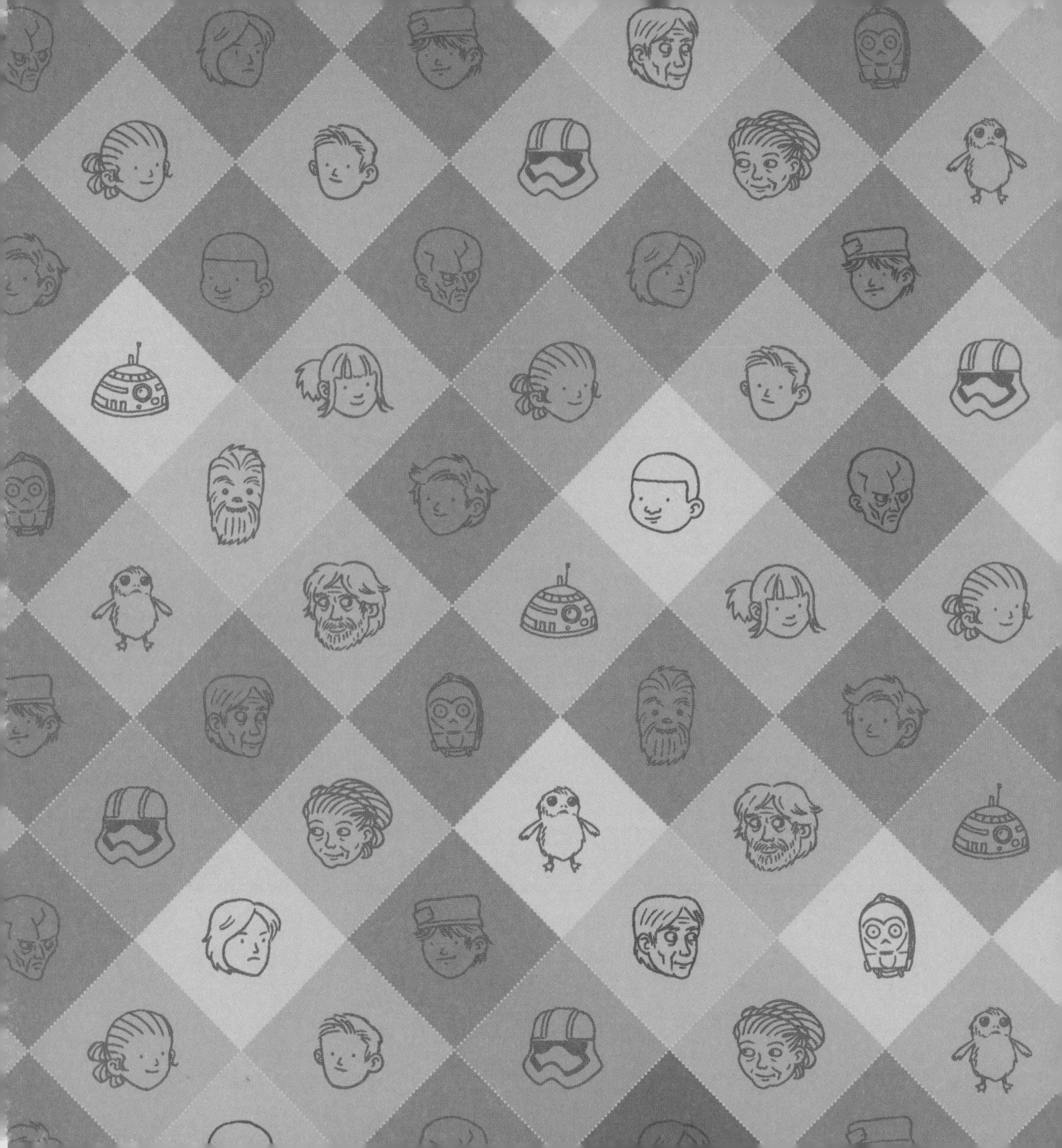